40 Powerful Thoughts for developing POSITIVE ATTITUDE

Emmanuel Anthony Das

PUSTAK MAHAL®

Publishers
Pustak Mahal®

Administrative office and sale centre

J-3/16 , Daryaganj, New Delhi-110002
☎ 23276539, 23272783, 23272784 • *Fax:* 011-23260518
E-mail: info@pustakmahal.com • *Website:* www.pustakmahal.com

Branches
Bengaluru: ☎ 080-22234025 • *Telefax:* 080-22240209
E-mail: pustakmahalblr@gmail.com
Mumbai: ☎ 022-22010941, 022-22053387
E-mail: unicornbooksmumbai@gmail.com
Patna: ☎ 0612-3294193 • *Telefax:* 0612-2302719
E-mail: rapidexptn@gmail.com

ISBN 978-81-223-1144-0
Edition: 2016

Price : ₹ 195/-

The book was earlier Printed under the title –
"The Best is Yet to Be"

Printed at : Arr Emm International, Delhi

Dedicated lovingly to

JOHN AND ELAINE
Thank you dear ones for
what you have done for me.

ACKNOWLEDGEMENTS

There are seven people whom I would like to thank personally from the bottom of my heart for their wonderful service, help and encouragement.

SPECIAL THANKS

1. God, the father in Heaven, Jesus Christ, Holy Mary, St. Anthony & All Saints.
2. My Parents – John Amala Das & Lourdes Emily.
3. My Sister – Manju & Prema Wilson.
4. My Mentor, Guide & Guru - Dr G Francis Xavier
5. My brothers – John, Gerard & Prabhu.
6. My Wife – Beena Joseph & Joel Anthony, my son .
7. My spiritual guides – the great Swami Vivekananda, Osho, Satya Sai Baba for their spiritual guidance.

I owe a deep sense of gratitude to all those who have been a source of inspiration and encouragement in my literary pursuit.

I am indebted to all the great writers from whom I have taken thoughts which have been added in my chapters. God bless them abundantly.

I thank all those who have been responsible for the publishing of this book, especially the ones whom I have not met, yet they have played a role in bringing this book to the shelves.

A word of special thanks GOES to the owners of Pustak Mahal. Thank you all for helping ME MAKE IT AGAIN!

CONTENTS

Preface 9

1. Humour 15
2. The Invisible Graph 22
3. God has His Own Ways 28
4. Great People Still Live 35
5. The River of Life 43
6. Better Late than Never 49
7. Be Careful, Always 56
8. Tough Times Never Last, Good Times Remain 63
9. Charity - A Great Deed 69
10. Hope Against Hope 75
11. Be Deaf, At Times 81
12. Grace Before Meals 87
13. Drop Things That Don't Work For You 93
14. God is There 99
15. Simply the Best 106
16. Life is a Gift 113
17. All for the Best 119
18. The Suffering Phase 126
19. Musings From a Millionaire 134
20. How to Stay Young 141

21. Thought is Another Name for Fate 147
22. Don't Think of People You Don't Like 153
23. Mistakes, A Part of Our Lives 159
24. Relationship - Visa to a Near One 165
25. Encourage Yourself 172
26. Attitude is Everything 178
27. Create a Heaven Within You 185
28. Be Sure There's a Problem 190
29. Failure 196
30. Moments in Life 203
31. Kindness Pays 209
32. Manage the Three- Time, Money and Thoughts 215
33. Leisure-Pleasure 222
34. Our Potential 229
35. Money is not Everything 235
36. Unburden Yourself 242
37. Love one Another 249
38. What to Do, What Not to Do 255
39. Know Your Destination 261
40. Stop Rewinding 267

PREFACE

Man lives on hopes and he waits that some good will happen to him. We must remember that '*the best is yet to be*'. It is always last to come for some, and hence we must wait for the best to come even if we have the best, we have to wait for the better.

As human beings we all live on hopes. Hope that we will do well in life. Many of us live in hope that we too will be living like a king one day and we keep our hopes alive till we reach the grave. But for some their dreams just come true. For many the dreams come true and in due course they vanish. But sadly, for some their hopes are just a pipe dream. They keep waiting and one day they too reach their final resting place. If we walk in the cemetery, there lies buried men and women, many who have had satisfied lives, many miserable lives, some the first half which was good and a miserable second half and for many a very bad and sad first half and thereby glorious days before they depart. All sleeping peacefully without any disturbance.

I fully believe if we have good days, they must last and not leave us lest we disintegrate. Man always goes by the adage '*the best is yet to be*'.

I always believe in this theory. Thanks to Arty Periera for that beautiful saying of hers. In every walk of life we have 'the best'. We speak about the best restaurant, the best travels, the best shirt, the best place to go for a holiday and so on. So what do you mean by that?

When a person achieves a certain amount of fame, he thinks that everything is over and that he has come to the end of the road. He must realise that there is a lot more to do as 'The Best is Yet to Be'. The person who invented the telephone did not realise how wonderful the instrument would be today. Unfortunately, he did not live to see it. He invented something shabby, heavy, not user friendly and that which was costly, but today man has improved upon it.

When my father was twelve-years-old, someone saw a car and commented that there would come a day where there would be modern cars which can fly. My father was a silent spectator when two people argued. One person said that it was possible. The other person said that it would not be possible. Probably the first person was right in what he said. Today, we have the Boeings and Airbuses which can house several hundreds of people and can fly at a very high altitude and at a great speed.

Today we have a very slim mobile phone from which you can speak, listen to music, send short messages, take photographs, store images and do a lot of things including calculations and fixing appointments. This is nothing but the great innovation that has taken place over the years.

The person who invents further and is doing such innovations has this beautiful theory 'The Best is Yet to Be', in mind otherwise we would have had the same old telephone.

If we look at cars too, we find the same innovation which it started from a rickety car where a lot of push was required. It has come to such a stage that we have the most modern cars with power steering, power windows, easy gear system, music, computers inbuilt, and several other modern methods to make driving comfortable.

When I say 'the best is yet to be', I mean there is still a lot more for anything in life. Take the example of a person learning English, he begins and is in a position to speak moderately. He must not think that everything is over. There is a lot more that he can do for himself. When it comes to general knowledge, there is a lot more for one to learn in life. No one can claim that he has a command over General Knowledge.

If you take any sphere of life, there is the best that can be achieved. But here, I would like to tell you in a lighter vein. This does not apply for wives and children. If one reads my book, he will be impressed with what I have written and will want to go for a better wife. Strictly, it is not allowed.

In every walk of life the best is yet to come. What we see today and think it as a very good, it will be called an antique someday. That is the result of modernisation. The good old Maruti car which was brought out in the early eighties is today an antique piece.

To sum up, let me tell you that you have to forge ahead in life always. Even if you get a Nobel Prize, do not stop there. You may feel that is the end, but there can be better ways where you can prove to the world that you can make it to the top. You have miles to go before you sleep.

At this juncture it is worth reading a poem by Robert Frost:

Whose woods these are I think I know.
His house is in the village though;
He will not see me stopping here
To watch his woods fill up with snow.
My little horse must think it queer
To stop without a farmhouse near
Between the woods and frozen lake
The darkest evening of the year.
He gives his harness bells a shake
To ask if there is some mistake.
The only other sound's the sweep
Of easy wind and downy flake.

The woods are lovely, dark and deep.
But I have promises to keep,
And miles to go before I sleep,
And miles to go before I sleep.

At the end of each chapter I have written as to how a particular topic can help in bettering yourself in life. That makes all the difference in the book. It runs into about 50 words but those 50 odd words can help you be the best of what you can be.

The Holy Quran says: 'Acquire knowledge. It enableth the possesors to distinguish right from wrong; it lighteth up the path of Heaven. It is our friend in the desert, our society in solitude, our companion when friendless. It guideth to happiness, it sustaineth in adversity. It is an ornament among friends, and an armour against enemies.'

THOUGHT

It was character that got us out of bed,
Commitment that moved us into action,
Discipline that enabled us to follow through.

STORY

Usually I take stories from sources, but in this case I have decided to give you, my readers my own story. It was the year 1995; I was down and out and was doing very bad in life. Every attempt that I made in business or work was a failure.

I did not know what to do. Finally I settled at one conclusion, and that is to wait and see what future had in store for me.

Little did I realise that the same year would be a turning point in my life. A certain friend of mine who was wealthy came to my house and began bragging about his opulence. He began by asking me where I was shopping for Christmas. I told him the question of shopping did not arise as I had no money even for three square meals.

I felt that he was boasting. That night, I kept pondering over what he said and began wondering if I could ever be in his place. I discussed this with a close friend of mine who is now in New Delhi and is doing very well in life. He told me that I had a lot of substance in me and that it was yet to come out. He also encouraged me and said that I had a lot of talent and that the same could be used for my growth.

He said, "Once you bring out your talent, you will be on top of the world and no one can bring you down." He added that the best in me was yet to be exposed to do wonders and marvels.

Today, I am in a very good position not just because of my friend's encouragement, but also because of my patience and way of thinking.

This book which you are reading is my seventh one.

THE BEST IS YET TO BE

Man lives on hope that he will see better days when he has good days. When he has his best days, he dreams further and that is 'the best is yet to be'. That is how we human beings are conditioned. We always hope for the better.

1

HUMOUR

There are three things which are real: God, human folly, and laughter. The first two are beyond our comprehension. So we must do what we can with the third on this hapless earth there's small sincerity of mirth and laughter oft is but an art to drown the outcry of the heart. As the crackling of thorns under a pot, so is laughter of the fool. Our sincerest laughter with some pain is fraught.

– Hartley Coleridge

Let me begin this book with a great humour. Humour as you know makes a lot of difference in one's life. All that I want to tell you is to laugh at the drop of a hat that will be nice for you and the others around you.

Laughter is the 'best medicine' and 'a smile can open any closed door'. It can calm nerves and bring about a sudden change in the other person's mind.

Humour opens the door to a pleasant relationship. Every day each of us has to face life anew. Every day we have to get out of bed, recharge our batteries and take on the challenges and pitfalls, promises and pain ahead of us. Anytime someone helps us laugh and feel better, we have a more appreciative attitude towards that person. Humour makes both the givers and the receivers feel better. It's as simple as that.

Late one night I was returning home from a dinner party. I was at Coimbatore at that time. While I was driving my car, I found a lot of barricades to slow down traffic due to two reasons. Private bus operators were very fast and rash in driving. The crime rate also is high in Coimbatore and the police wanted to check that. I was driving quite fast listening to music. Suddenly I realised that I was caught at the wrong side of the barricade when I barged inside the area in spite of a bus giving me a signal to wait. The opposite side had a government bus driven by an elderly driver.

He jammed brakes and almost got a heart attack when he saw me right in front of him. He looked out to shout at me and asked me to reverse my car. Even before I reversed my car I peeped out, waved out and smiled and shouted, 'I am sorry, extremely sorry.' In the beginning he looked upset, but when he saw me dressed neatly and that too with pleasant manners, he returned the smile and went on his way. I felt I had done the right thing, rather than throwing my weight around. Hence I say, 'A smile will cost you nothing, it can win friends and bring people close to you.'

Humour in life is all about living life rather than merely surviving it and enjoying everything one is associated with. Also one has to experience excitement in all achievements and has to blossom into a flower that can be admired. One should prefer to laugh at times, at failure also. One has to keep the 'sense of discovery' alive.

Types of Humour

There are three types. They are:

1. Compassionate Humour
2. Caustic Humour and
3. Unhealthy Humour.

Compassionate Humour: Compassionate humour helps to bridge the gaps between people, break tension, provide hope and increase positivity in a situation. It is accepting, mature and healing and beneficial to our health.

Caustic Humour: When humour is used in such a way that feelings of hostility, distress and general negativity are aroused. It is called caustic humour. For example, putting someone down or excluding them all together. Children and teenagers often use this though it can also be seen in adults at times.

Unhealthy Humour: Most of us have experienced situations where people crack jokes on our weakness. We feel embarrassed, humiliated and resentful towards the person who tells the joke and towards all the people who are laughing at the joke.

Importance of Humour

Do you want to move 72 muscles in you or 16 muscles in your face? Laughter guarantees minimum use of muscles in your face. A simple 'U curve' in your mouth straightens things.

Benefits of Humour

Laughter invokes feeling of happiness and joy. Under conditions of happiness, joy and merriment it is much easier to think creatively around a problem than when our mind is filled with a sense of helplessness, worthlessness and inadequacies.

Shared laughter promotes harmony and unity within a group. People feel more welcome and free to offer suggestions and think out loud. They are not afraid of being put down, so they take the risk of sharing their opinions. Humour is hazardous to illness. If a humorous comment is made and expresses the concerns in an exaggerated way, people will laugh. By laughing an entry is made to talk about the subject.

Laughter appears to reduce levels of certain stress hormones. It acts as a safety valve that shuts off the flow of stress hormones.

Stress hormones suppress the immune system, increase the number of platelets (which can cause obstruction in arteries) and raise blood pressure. Laughter boosts the immune system. When you are in a state of happiness, natural killer cells that destroy tumours and viruses increase. It also increases the concentration of salivary immunoglobulin which defends against the entry of infectious organisms through the respiratory track.

A man who always sees the funny side of any situation can never be a pessimist. Laughter is inner jogging and is good for a person's cardio vascular system. Humour is contagious and others around you too immediately respond.

Why humour in life?

It supports the emotional stability. It enhances the urge to do more in life. It encourages taking up bigger challenges in life. It supports longevity and dilutes stress. It helps build better relationships which in turn promotes higher acceptance. It will make one a very successful team worker. It makes one commit more (When there is a greater job satisfaction, the executive of a company will dare to take up bigger challenges). It reduces boredom and fatigue, which in turn kicks off the excitement curve towards higher goals and greater rewards.

A very powerful way is to carry with you that BIG SMILE which always opens doors – minds and hearts. Humour has a therapeutic value which stems from that old saying:

'Laughter is the best medicine.'

How to acquire a sense of Humour?

One should accept the world as it is. Search any scope for humour in your day to day life. Point out the errors in a humorous manner. Use humour as a tool rather than as a weapon. Collect cartoons, jokes and keep them in a separate file for future reference. Stick them up in the most stressful places in your house, for example; your desk, your cupboard, your mirror or your dressing table. Join mailing lists that send jokes and funny anecdotes regularly. At least set apart half an hour every week to watch a humorous serial/movie.

Make sure you genuinely laugh once or twice a day. Attend any conference/ seminar on humour whenever it is held. Learn to appreciate all good things in life. Also be in a positive frame of mind always.

STORY

There is a story of an Irishman who was known all over for his humour and wit but he died suddenly and went up for the divine judgement. He was feeling extremely uneasy. He didn't think he had done much good on earth! There was a queue ahead of him so he settled to listen and look.

After consulting his big book, God said to the first man in the queue 'I see here that I was hungry and you gave me food to eat, good man! Go to heaven' to the second man he sent to heaven as well as he had given him water when he was thirsty and the third man was also sent to heaven as this man had gone to visit him when he was sick. And so it went on.

The Irishman now sat examining his conscience and felt he had a great deal to fear. He had never given anyone food or water or visited any sick person. But, when his turn came.....

The Irishman was also sent to heaven, because God said that whenever He was depressed and felt discouraged this man's timely jokes and funny stories made Him laugh and be happy.

Jokes make people laugh. Laughter brings happiness and good health. In this way people who advocate and practise wit and humour do a lot of service to humanity.

Humour

The local news station was interviewing an 80-year-old lady because she had just got married - for the fourth time.

The interviewer asked her questions about her life, about what it felt like to be marrying again at 80, and then about her new husband's occupation.

'He's a funeral director,' she answered 'Interesting,' the newsman thought.

He then asked her if she wouldn't mind telling him a little about her first three husbands and what they did for a living.

She paused for a few moments, needing time to reflect on all those years.

After a short time, a smile came to her face and she answered proudly, explaining that she'd first married a banker when she was in her early 20's, then a circus ringmaster when in her 40's, later on a preacher when in her 60's, and now in her 80's, a funeral director.

The interviewer looked at her, quite astonished, and asked why she had married four men with such diverse careers.

She smiled and explained, 'I married the first one for the money, second for the show, third to get ready, and fourth to go.'

THOUGHT

May your thoughts be of flowers?
May your dreams be of love?
May the stars twinkling down on us be your ever guiding love?
May you find hope in all your fear and fright?
May you find love that is only heard through the whispers of the night?
May we love one another and lose this fight
May we all be equal in each other's sight?
May our tears be kissed away by hope and of wisdom?
God may give the courage to give love in all I do
May you love yourself and others too?

God has Humour

God was in the process of creating the universe. And He was explaining to His subordinates, 'Look everything should be in balance. For example, after every 10 deer there should be a lion.'

Look here my fellow angels; here is the country of the United States. I have blessed them with prosperity and money. But at the same time I have given them insecurity and tension. And here in Africa, I have given them beautiful nature. But at the same time, I have given them climatic extremes.

And here is South America. I have given them lots of forests. But at the same time, I have given them lesser land so that they would have to cut off the forests. So you see fellows, everything should be in balance.

One of the angels asked. 'God, what is this extremely beautiful country here?'

God said, "Aha! That is the crown of my creation – India, my most precious creation. It has understanding and friendly people. Sparkling streams and serene mountains. A culture which speaks of the great tradition that they live. Technologically brilliant and with a heart of gold."

The angel was quite surprised: 'But God you said everything should be in balance.' God replied – 'Look at the neighbours, I gave them.'

THE BEST IS YET TO BE

Where humour is concerned, what I would like to tell and share with you is, you may be down and out with worries and tensions, but if you smile a while in spite of all these problems, I am sure something better is yet to come.

◆◆◆

2

THE INVISIBLE GRAPH

Most of us do not know about the invisible graph that we carry along with us. As we do good the good graph goes up. When we do some bad, the bad graph goes up. When it comes to a judgement, what matters is not money wealth, power or position, but it is the graph which is larger. That matters.

No one knows if the law of nemesis prevails or not. We hear people say he is doing bad in life because of 'karma' his past actions. It is not proved scientifically that a person can make atonement in the present life for the sins committed in the previous birth. We find beggars who beg and lead miserable lives. Of course you will find beggars who also live in luxuries.

Whenever we see a beggar, we will say, 'He is such a miserable creature; he has surely been a past sinner in the previous life. We tell the same with a man who is poor and is leading a hard life.' Great philosophers have mooted the idea of retribution which they say prevails in all our lives. That is we have an invisible graph within us, that indicates the good and the bad we do. The size of the graph will constitute what we will become or how we have a life. The negative graph is on the higher side, we will have a bad life and if the positive graph is on the higher side, we will have a smooth sailing in life.

It is also believed that if the negative graph is big, it will be as heavy as iron, but if the positive graph is big, it will be as light as a feather. That is why people who are struggling may be the ones who have the big negative graph and have great difficulty to carry themselves easily. The ones who have the big positive graph will not only walk with ease but will also walk freely without any difficulty.

If you look at the life of man, he does two things. One is the good and the other is the bad deeds in life. Most often we tend to fool around with people and get away with money power, using musclemen or doing something that is not good for both us and the others. You must remember there is something existing in the law of nature called 'nemesis' which will not spare any one, be it a minister, doctor, lawyer or anybody for that matter.

I am referring to the good and the bad we do in life. While many of us are unconscious about the bad that we do, we still continue to do it in spite of knowing pretty well that a certain thing is wrong. A man who kills animals says that he is doing for his livelihood; he does not realise the pain he is bringing to an animal or bird. He simply does it as a part of his duty.

Same is the case with a soldier, who kills his enemy in spite of knowing that the enemy soldier is also a human being with emotions and also loved by his family, but for the moment the soldier who is out to kill his enemy knows only one thing and that is to kill his enemy. His bad graph will go up drastically.

There is an invisible graph behind our backs which we all carry without knowing about it. It is similar to that of our bank account where we keep our money in safe custody. When we remove money from the bank the balance goes down, when we deposit the money the balance goes up. Same is the case with the good and the bad that we do in our lives.

There are two graphs on either side of the shoulder. On the right is the graph for the good deeds that we do in our lives. On the left side of the shoulder is the graph for the bad deeds that we do. As the deeds are done, the graph goes up. We have made a study and got a ratio of people based on what we spoke to them and found out about their background.

1. Good Graph 20 Bad Graph 80
2. Good Graph 80 Bad Graph 20
3. Good Graph 10 Bad Graph 90
4. Good Graph 90 Bad Graph 10
5. Good Graph 05 Bad Graph 95
6. Good Graph 98 Bad Graph 02
7. Good Graph 02 Bad Graph 98

On studying we find that many people are not aware of the fact that they have these invisible charts behind them. Many people refuse to believe in such a theory existing. There are also some who blindly believe in what we say and assure us that they will change their way of living.

A word of caution to the ones whose good graph is high; continue to do what you are doing unmindful of what is happening in the neighbourhood. Don't get carried away by what is being done by others, if you are doing good you continue to do it.

At the same time I am addressing the ones whose bad deeds have an upper hand. All you can do is to learn lessons before it is too late and get your good graph going up rather than increasing your bad one up. We believe in the saying 'the evil you do remains with you, the good you do comes back to you'. This is very true in many cases.

I still remember as a child, we all lived in a joint family. Our grandmother who was the head of the family and earned great respect was the one who commanded all of us like the army general. My grandfather was concentrating on the intellectual side and would keep reading more and keep to himself, while my grandmother would concentrate on the upbringing and managing the family. On one occasion a man named 'Natraj' who worked with our family to do errand jobs was coming into our compound. She looked at him and asked, 'Why are you late?' He smiled and said, 'Last night, I slept late and hence I woke up late this morning.' It was a Sunday. My grandmother told him to go and fetch milk. He took the aluminium can and ran out.

As he left, my grandmother commented, 'This man is struggling in life, he has a bad health, he is partially lame and has a hunch, but still he does not want to leave his drinking habit.' She then commented to her sister and said, 'It looks like this man would have been a very arrogant and would have committed a lot of sins in his previous birth, that is why is paying for all that in this life.'

What my grandmother said was very meaningful, all that the others did was to remain silent and not to comment. We did not know why she made such a statement, but the same man had a very serious accident and died on the road. He died at the same spot where a dog had died the previous day. We all felt sad that the man who served our family had fallen on the road and died and that too on a par with a dog. What a life?

To sum up, now that I have told you about the graphs, what have you decided? Turn a new leaf today and begin to do only good things in life rather than engage in bad deeds. After all, remember you derive joy in doing well. You don't get any pleasure when you harm someone. You are at the miserable end and the other person also suffers as a result.

The great emperor Asoka said; 'What matters in life is not a person's status or position, but his virtues and wisdom.' The finest minds and hearts may be hidden in ugly mortal frames. Only when you have realised yourself, can you recognise the greatness of a few in a sea of humanity, just as a good jeweller alone can spot a gem among worthless pebbles.

THOUGHT

The Greatest Things

- The best day - **Today**
- The best gift - **Forgiveness**
- The meanest feeling - **Jealousy**
- The greatest need - **Commonsense**
- The most expensive indulgence - **Hate**
- The greatest trouble maker - **Talking Too Much**
- The cleverest man - **One who does what he thinks right**
- The greatest teacher - **One who makes you want to learn**
- The worst bankrupt - **The soul that has lost enthusiasm**
- The cheapest, stupidest, **easiest thing to do - Finding fault**
- The best part of one's religion - **Gentleness & Cheerfulness.**

STORY

A wealthy lady became inordinately proud of her fine mansion and landscaped garden. She was an avowed materialist. Her faithful old gardener looked at everything so differently. Despite his poverty, he saw the world as a wonderful place, full of beautiful simple things-the flowers he tended, the birds who serenaded him at work, the delicacy of scudding clouds. From his pittance he was always ready to help where he could.

The lady died, and as she looked around heaven for her rightful abode she was directed to a mean, tumble-down shack. 'I think you have made a mistake' she said, 'I've always been used to something really worthy. I had a charming house – sixteen rooms – luxurious, the best that money could buy.'

Then spotting a delightful dwelling close by, nearing completion, she brightened. 'Ah, now, what about that one? That's the sort of place I'd like.'

'Sorry Madam, you can't have that; we are getting that ready for your gardener when he comes.'

'My gardener? But he's used to a tiny cottage: why couldn't you prepare one like that for me?'

And the celestial housing officer replied; 'Impossible, Madam. It's right out of our hands; we can only build with the materials sent up by the future occupants. He's sent us magnificent material, always, yours was a bit substandard, you must admit.' It is not the material possessions but right attitudes to life that matter a lot for success and happiness.

THE BEST IS YET TO BE

Where the invisible graph is concerned, you can be assured that if you would have done well in the past, it is likely to help you. If you are in bad times, just wait, good times will come.

◆◆◆

3

GOD HAS HIS OWN WAYS

God is in corporal, divine, supreme, infinite mind, spirit, soul, principle, life, truth and love. God is not a cosmic bell-boy for whom we can press a button to get things done. God is love and He dwelleth in love. God is supreme and He is above all and can do what He wishes which no one can question. God is above time and space.

The one thing I must tell you about God is that He is above all of us and I believe in His existence even though I have not seen Him. But I can vouch that I have heard Him speak to me. My first God on earth is my mother and my second God is my father, of course I would fail in my responsibility if I do not mention about the God, the father in Heaven whom I love, depend, worship, pray and revere. All said and done, He is there and He is blessing me abundantly and is looking after all my needs without any reservation like how a mother does to her children.

This statement of mine may be a little contradicting but what I have to say about God's plan is He has His own ways of doing things, He causes famine in one place and gives extra grains in another. He denies water at one place and sends floods in another place. That is God's own plan. No one can question the authority of God. He is the master and we have to live by what he does.

God creates beggars who have no assured food. He also creates millionaires who have so much food and can throw plenty to dogs and swines. No one can question God about it. But God gives every man an opportunity. It is left to man to take it or leave it. Some people whom we call clever take the opportunity, while others do not take it and either say that they are unlucky or that they are waiting for the big day to come. Finally such people land up in poverty and at times do not leave behind money even for their funeral.

God takes man into deep waters to cleanse and never to drown him. We cannot question the authority of God. He will do what he feels like. If you look at the world, you will see the lame, the blind, the insane, the maniac, the midget, and the abnormal ones and so on and so forth. All these people are also creations of God. But why are they the way they are?

We cannot question God. For that matter even if you want to question God, how do you get an appointment and where do you meet him. A close friend of mine who took up the job of a pastor (because he did not get any other job) went to see God, he is yet to return. No trace of him, so sad.

Some people are born blind. Some are lame. Some others are even deaf. You will also find many people who are perpetual patients. Some people fall sick at the drop of a hat. On the other side you have people who are very rich. Many people are wealthy, but on the other side you have people who are in the middle segment. You will also find people who are on the hand to mouth living. Let us not forget the poorest of the poor. Why are people in such categories? They are all children of God.

God I am sure has his own ways. He knows what to do and what not to do. There is one theory that is doing the rounds and that is karma. Some people believe in karma. If you ask me if I believe in karma, I will keep quiet. As I have no idea about it. Sometimes I am forced to believe it, at times I feel it is not there as our God is a merciful God and He will not want to take revenge on the same men He created.

I have an atheist friend who mocks at me when I speak about God. He is very critical about people building Churches, Temples and spending money for festivals and offerings to God. I agree with him on certain counts, but I am forced to respect the views of brothers and sisters of India. I find no fault with any caste, creed or religion. Each one has got his own likes and dislikes and one must be given the freedom to do what he wants to do.

We must understand one thing about God. He can do what He wants. We cannot question His authority. He can give a life, He can take a life or He can even break a marriage. He has his own ways. At times I too get angry with God, but then again I feel it is of no use getting angry with our own creator. If I look at what I have with me today, I just ignore what I do not have and hence I am satisfied that He has His own ways. Some time ago I lost a very good friend of mine, young dashing and dynamic. He had helped me during my difficult days. He has left behind a young widow and two young children. I was upset with God but then again I cannot question His will and ways. I just thanked Him that I was alive.

STORY

Remaud was a French senator who had rented a hotel room for a month and paid in advance all the money due. The hotelkeeper asked him if he wanted the cash receipt.

'Oh, don't bother,' said the senator. 'It is enough that God has seen it.'

'Why monsieur, you believe in God?' asked the hotelkeeper.

'Of course and you do too, don't you?'

'No sir, I don't.'

The senator said: 'On a second thought I feel that I should have a receipt from you.'

Fear of God brings discipline in a person. Strong belief in the presence of God would make a person to be more sincere, honest and truthful. In the absence of such reverential fear one may be tempted to do all types of anti-social activities. This is the main reason for all religions to propound the theory of the existence of one God.

At this juncture it is worth remembering a beautiful saying:

I was in blues
For I had no shoes
Till I saw a man with no feet.

I grumbled as I did not get a ray ban sunglass, till my mother held my hand and took me to a place where the blind could not see. I then realised what my mother said.

'Be satisfied with whatever you have.'

God will give you a sunny day one day.
He will send torrent rains another day.
He will flood cities and towns in one place.
He will send famine in another region.
He has his own way of doing things.
These are acts of God. I believe it is a signal from God to say 'Be careful.'
God leads you to the edge of a cliff and will let you go.

Two things will happen.

He will either catch you when you fall.

Or he will teach you to fly.

Hence we have to trust in God.

Poem

O God, help me to find myself.
Help me, oh God, in the quest of life.
To find myself.
As I pass through the ivory gates of morning.
And the ebon doors of night.
Let beauty make me aware.
For with the passport of personality
Have I set sail on the vast deep of destiny?
To gather the glistering fruit of self-culture
The attar and mirth of friendship
And the fine gold of character
Persuaded that the beleaguered soul
Surrenders only to thee.

God said, 'No.'

I hope that you can get the effects on your computers! The words are great, but the movements of the faces add a lot...

I asked God to take away my habit.

God said, 'No. It is not for me to take away, but for you to give it up.'

I asked God to make my handicapped child whole.

God said, 'No. His spirit is whole, his body is only temporary.'

I asked God to grant me patience.

God said, 'No. Patience is a by-product of tribulations; it isn't granted, it is learned.'

I asked God to give me happiness.

God said, 'No. I give you blessings; Happiness is up to you.'

I asked God to spare me pain.

God said, 'No. Suffering draws you apart from worldly cares and brings you closer to me.'

I asked God to make my spirit grow.

God said, 'No. You must grow on your own, but I will prune you to make you fruitful.'

I asked God for all things that I might enjoy life.

God said, 'No. I will give you life, so that you may enjoy all things.'

I asked God to help me love others, as much as He loves me.

God said, 'Ahhhh, finally you have the idea.'

As I close this chapter, I would like to advise my readers to remember God in every walk of your life, pray to Him, plead with Him, seek His help at all times and above all believe that He can work wonders for you. Do not forget, God has His own ways and He can do what He wants, it is He who decides what is good for us and what is not. We must not question His existence, we must not fume when we do not get what we want, we have to wait patiently for He is our maker and knows what to give us and what not to give. A little patience will help us in the long run, I too was frustrated with God and soon I realised that He loved me and wanted me to have what I wanted. I shall go back to Him satisfied, content and happy that He gave me such a beautiful opportunity to live life.

THE BEST IS YET TO BE

Where man is put to sufferings, he struggles and curses God and also people around him. Little does he know that there is a great amount of good that is going to come for him. The best will always come last for some.

◆◆◆

4

GREAT PEOPLE STILL LIVE

The great men who have walked on this earth have died physically, but we still remember their faces and also their works and hence it becomes the duty of every person to do what these great people have done for the world.we still talk about them, we take their examples and we have also constructed memorials and statues for these great men.

When we talk about death, what do we mean? The physical body of a person is dead and gone. We either bury the dead or burn it. Some great people like Industrialist Ravi Kirloskar and Jyoti Basu, the Marxist leader of West Bengal have also donated their cadavers for research purposes. Death may occur for some people but some people die and yet they live long after they are dead physically and have gone. What I mean here is for great people there is only physical death, but yet they are immortal and live in our hearts and minds.

Whenever I conduct a workshop, people ask me what is the picture of Swami Vivekananda doing here. I have a standee which has got my own photo with my saying which reads as follows:

In order to succeed in life,
one has to trust the immense potential
that is hidden inside.

Next to that is the picture of Swami Vivekananda, whom I acknowledge as my 'role model.' One of his famous sayings is:

'Man is the maker of his destiny.'

I have made it a point to speak about Swamiji in all my sessions as he is the person who has impressed me very much after my father, the difference is my father is living physically and is in my heart always and Swamiji is also in my heart, but his physical body is not there. His spirit guides me, I feel that swamiji is still living somewhere in some planet.

I will list out eight great men who have lived on this earth and have left their footprints on the sands of time. They are:

1. Jesus Christ - *Spirituality*
2. Gautama Buddha - *Religion*
3. Thomas Alva Edison - *Inventions*
4. Alexander the Great – *Strategist and Conqueror*
5. William Shakespeare - *Literature*
6. Nostradamus - *Prediction*
7. Subhash Chandra Bose – *Freedom Fighter*
8. Mother Teresa – *Charity*

We are fortunate to live during the time of these great men. Such great people who still live and will go down in history some years down the line are:

1. Satya Sai Baba
2. Bill Gates
3. Sonia Gandhi
4. Mohammed Ali

5. Rakesh Sharma
6. Rajesh Khanna
7. Kapil Dev.

Great Religious Leaders of India

1. Swami Vivekananda
2. Adi Shankara
3. Aurobindo
4. Ramkrishna Paramhamsa
5. Guru Nanak
6. Mahaveera
7. Gautama Buddha.

Philosophers

1. Rajneesh
2. Jiddu Krishnamurthy
3. Subramanya Bharathi
4. Rajgopalachari
5. Sarvapalli Radhakrishnan
6. Lokmanya Bal GangadharTilak
7. Rabindranath Tagore.

Some time ago India was written off in the field of sports. But in any country there are geniuses who make the nation proud and we in India have also had the privilege of having such great people who have proved to the world **'with a little effort, confidence and courage, we can move the mountains'**. And such great people who have toiled and shown the way to the youngsters of the country are listed below.

Some of the great sports legends whose names will go down in history are:

1. Milkha Singh

2. Kapil Dev
3. P T Usha
4. Geet Sethi
5. Prakash Padukone
6. Leander Paes
7. Dhyanchand

Till the late eighties India was termed as a poor and an under-developed country. But of late India has shot to the internatioanal limelight with some great men stealing the show at the international level. These great men have made India proud. The younger generation can take a clue from these great people and can also achieve wonders and marvels. We salute these great Indian men who have proved, **'If others have done it, why can't we?'**

Great Business Leaders of India

1. J R D Tata – Tata Group
2. G D Birla – Birla Group
3. Dhirubai Ambani - Reliance
4. Lakshmi Mittal – Mittal Steel
5. Azim Premji - Wipro
6. Narayana Murthy - Infosys
7. Ramlinga Raju – Satyam

People who have entertained millions in India and rest of the world and who have contributed to the field of arts are these people who are listed below. They have proved that we in India can have a Beethoven and also have a James Last. What we learn from these Indian geniuses are that 'nothing is impossible', **with determination, smart work and love for your profession, we can make things work**.

Indian geniuses who have excelled and made India proud at the International level are:

1. Lata Mangeskar
2. Ilaiyaraaja
3. R D Burman
4. Pandit Ravishankar
5. Hari Prasad Chaurasia
6. Zakir Hussain
7. Kishore Kumar

There are also many people who are toiling day and night and to ensure that people in India get justice. They have no ambitions, nor vie for luxuries. They risk their lives and fight for the rights of the poor, displaced and justice-denied persons. They all say with one voice **'all men must have equal rights to live peacefully in society, no matter who they are and which area or religion they belong to'**.

1. Arundhati Roy
2. Baba Amte
3. Medha Patkar
4. Teesta Setalvad
5. Shabana Azmi
6. Shantha Sinha
7. Rajkumari Amrit Kaur

That brings me to the question. Are great men born or are they created, or for that matter does one just become one with courage, conviction and contribution? I feel that most great men did not know that they would become great. There are some who had a vision to become great someday and hence we remember them. I sum up this chapter by stating that all of you who read this book can become great and leave your footprints on the sands of time. To become great it is not necessary that you be a member of a royal family. All you need is to have is determination to succeed and do something which the world will follow and remember you for the rest of time.

THOUGHT

Her perseverance is laudable.
Through perseverance anything can be achieved.

By trying again and again even the most stubborn vice can be removed and virtues can be developed.

If you try again and again nothing is impossible for you to achieve. This virtue of perseverance is one of the hallmarks of all great achievers on this planet.

'If you wish success in life make perseverance your bosom friend, experience your counsellor, caution your elder brother and hope your guardian angel.'

— Joseph Addison

Qualities of Great Men

Sir Isaac Newton called Diamond by his side and said, 'Diamond, little do you know the trouble and labour to which you have put your master.' Then he did not look upon that great work as lost forever like most people would have done. He sat down at his desk to start all over again.

Patience is the key to success. A person who is emotionally aroused is unable to make a good judgement and often loses contact with reality. Contrarily, persons of substance have the ability to straighten out their emotional life and are thus able to use their intelligence to the highest degree. They remain calm in emergencies and are not easily provoked. That is why they are able to co-ordinate their ideal with concrete reality.

STORY

Philomen and Bausis were a very loving couple. They had a son who was away in a foreign country and sent money for their maintenance. The couple were very kind and helpful and served the entire village folk. As time grew the old man began planting trees and his wife began watering them. They planted trees that provided shade, fruits and other edible items like tamarind.

The people of the village often wondered why they were doing such a thing when they would not live to see the trees grow and give them fruits. The old man said, 'We may not live, but we are planting for our future generations.'

Soon the old lady died and left the old man in the lurch. The old man was bed-ridden, but he had a host of village folk who were ready to look after him. Unable to bear the loss of his beloved wife the old man too died. The entire village mourned the death of the two great people.

Women on one side took the old woman as their role model and began helping the others in distress. The same went with many men of the village who followed what the old man had done.

The village was not what it was, it became a very shady place with a lot of fruit bearing trees. The place was cool and the villagers were in a position to grow crops and vegetables. Soon the entire patch became a mini forest.

The names of the couple were written on stone. Every household remembered them. A huge memorial was constructed for the couple. This memorial has a shelter for travellers. It also had a lot of trees and plants on all sides. It was a wonderful place, a paradise on earth. This place which was barren, dry and desolated got its look from the great couple who set an example.

Great people never knew that they would become great some day. They did great things that made them so. Unfortunately we do not rememebr all the great people who have lived in this world. We remember only a few. The amount of great people who lived in this world and have passed away runs into several millions. We remember only those who are famous and were brought to the notice of people. We have had so many people who have given us so many inventions that it may amount to several millions, even though we cannot do anything for them we can at least be grateful and maintain some silence in their memory.

What makes a person great? When he does some good for society, a person becomes great among men.

THE BEST IS YET TO BE

If you have not decided to become great, do it today. We talk so much about great people and glorify them. If you become great, one day people will talk good about you too. Becoming great is a virtue which is given to all.

◆◆◆

5

THE RIVER OF LIFE

The river of life flows free and is fair to all. Anyone who desires to have wholesome life can go to the river with a barrel and not a small can for one can fill as much as he wants to have for his life upliftment. The river of life flows all over and is at times invisible, it is visible only to those who seek it.

When God created man, He had great ideas about his future and also conduct in life on earth. Unfortunately, God got a shock of his life when man protested and turned hostile towards the very God that created him. There are three types of people on this earth today.

They are:

1. People who love God
2. People who do not love God
3. People who love God at times and hate Him at times.

People Who Love God: These are the type of people are God-fearing and have love for God. They practise and follow religion and are very pious and good-hearted by nature. Unfortunately, we find very few people in this category. Originally, God wanted to have such people, but somehow He was in for a shock when men protested and turned hostile. That is how Satan has influenced people and have taken them into his fold. It is sad to see the world disintegrating and going down these days.

Status - *Such people are happy internally, externally. Many of them may be happy.*

People Who Do Not Love God: The people who commit sin and do what is said that 'we must not do' in the holy scriptures like the Bible, Granth, Koran or the Vedas, fall under this category. Politicians, rowdy elements, financiers, people doing business and cheating people fall under this category. There is also one more important category of people who are so-called preachers and gurus who are famous. But their fame and name does not suit them to be holy people. They are the representatives of Satan on earth.

Status - *Such people may have wealth and opulence, but internally they suffer a lot, but they do not show it to others.*

People who love God at times and hate Him at times: These are the people whom I call time-servers. Such people go to God when they are in dire need and ignore God when they are doing well. They go to God at the last moment for something and if God does not give them what they ask for, they term God as either bad or non-existent. Such people seldom do well in life, most of them struggle in life, those few people who have success are also the ones who are not happy in life.

Status – *Only a few people are happy internally, some happy externally, but they shuttle between the good and the bad, they land up very unhappy in life.*

Life itself is a gift of God wherein we have to live life to the fullest and best and go back after we have achieved a lot on this earth. Man is the only creature that is endowed with the gift of laughter and the sixth sense which no other living being has. In view of this we have to laugh and enjoy our lives and also use our sixth sense to do constructive things and not invent things that will cause destruction.

Let us take the example of the man who invented the atom and nuclear bomb, his main aim was to see that the world was vanquished in a short span of time and that too in the most gorgeous manner.

We all have opportunities in abundance that is given to us in equality. Time is available for twenty four hours. This twenty four hours is given to a beggar, millionaire as well as common man. Even the President of America and the Prime Minister of India have only twenty four hours. They are not greater than any beggar or a miserable person on earth. This is one aspect where mother nature is reasonable to all.

Another factor that I would like to touch upon is 'fame' which we all know. There is one thing which we all must know about fame. All of us are not passionate with fame. Only some of us are to become famous. This aspect is also available to all of us living on this earth. Whoever you are, a beggar, a business tycoon, an actor, a mason, a scientist or a criminal serving a jail term – all of us are free to go after fame. Why is that only some people become famous? Some go after fame and achieve it and some become famous automatically. Some people have become famous because of certain people making them famous.

Life has got a lot of things to offer, it offers us a lot of good things. It offers all these things to all unmindful of who we are where we live. It does not see any region, gender, religion and age.

They are:

1. Name
2. Fame
3. Popularity
4. Wealth
5. Power
6. Cosy Life
7. Happiness.

Name: To get a name we don't need to be born in a particular caste, creed, religion or a family. All we need to have is a burning desire to get a name for ourself and we will get it if we proceed towards it.

Fame: Fame is not the birthright of any person. Anyone who does something differently becomes famous. There is nothing called luck in fame, it is only a good timing and an eagerness to do so.

Popularity: If one does something unique or some crime he gains popularity. Great men in the world became popular. Anyone who does something good becomes popular, again popularity can come for anyone whoever he may be.

Wealth: Many people are born rich. Some people become rich after they get money. Those people who are born rich, will surely have ancestors who might have worked hard. Wealth can be created by anyone. It only takes a little effort and smart work in getting wealth.

Power: Unfortunately today we have the wrong people in power. More than ninety per cent of the people who are in power today are either power-hungry and come to power through nefarious means or are the wrong persons. Coming to power is also very easy, it requires a little crooked traits.

Cosy Life: Some people have a very cosy life like cats. These people do not toil and get everything they want in life. They don't have to work for anything. All that they have is opulence, luxuries and money which can bring them anything they want.

Happiness: Hapiness is something that all are not endowed upon. Only a few people are fortunate to have happiness in life. It is not just money, name or fame that matters, but even a man who is without riches can have happiness. Happiness is something which we have to create and cannot buy.

Anyone wanting the above seven aspects can go after it, no man was born rich or for that matter the seven points are not the birthright of any particular community, caste or gender.

Similarly life also offers us bad or negative things. This offer like the good ones is open. Anyone can go after it and take it.

They are:

1. Pain
2. Disease
3. Poverty
4. Failures
5. Social Stigmas
6. Rejections
7. Snubbing

Pain: Some people are born with pain and continue to live in pain. The worst part is when a person is in pain, he does not get it on his own. Another person who is not in pain inflicts this pain on him.

Disease: Some people are born with diseases and suffer from it all their life. I have seen one thing in people who suffer from diseases. It is in their mind that the disease cannot be removed, they come out with a lot of theories for suffering like karma, bad deeds done in previous birth etc.

Poverty: People who live in the slums can also live in apartments if they desire, but they fix their minds that only certain people are destined to live in flats and hence they continue to live in slums.

Failures: Failure does not spare anybody, it is a part of life. Many people fail in life and take them very seriously in life and go to the grave with miseries. A person who fails must realise that there is still hope for him.

Social Stigmas: This is one area which cannot be banished, especially in a country like ours. All that one can do is to achieve something great and gain name and fame for himself.

Rejections: In every walk of life we face rejections, it can be at school, at an interview; it could be a marriage proposal or it could be at home. We must be ready to take rejection with a positive outlook. I have heard many people ending lives because of rejection which is totally wrong.

Snubbing: Snubbing happens to man day in and day out. We just take snubbing with a positive outlook rather than fret and fume and take revenge on the person who snubs us. We have to identify why we have been snubbed and take measures to correct ourselves.

The most important thing that one must realise where his life is concerned is that he must know what is good for him and what is not good for him. That is because if you enter the area of life deeply it will be difficult to exit. Recently a friend of mine who was doing very bad in life approached me for counselling.

When I told him to change his line of activity, he simply said, 'I am forty years of age and it is too late to do something new.'

Another example is a person who was an anti-national element was captured by the Government forces. When they questioned him to reform himself he said, 'I cannot transform as I may be killed by my gang members.'

THE BEST IS YET TO BE

The barrel of life is available for all of us. Those of us who have not seen sunshine in life can go to the barrel of life and fill it up to the brim so that we can have a wonderful life, after all the barrel of life is free for all.

◆◆◆

6

BETTER LATE THAN NEVER

We have to realise that even if we go a little late we still manage to get a shouting from someone or people may even mistake us if we are superior to them. Is that not better than starting late and hurrying and taking a risk? This risk is not only going to bring doom for us but it also brings doom to those who are depending on us.

I have seen many drivers of cars, buses and other vehicles taking time for granted. They suddenly realise that they have only some time left to reach a particular place. The easiest way for them is to go fast and reach the place. When they do this, they risk their own lives, the lives of passengers and co-workers.

The chances of danger in bigger vehicles are very less compared to the smaller ones when they are negligent. I have personally seen a driver smoking and sipping tea slowly, suddenly the bus conductor put pressure on him and he got into the bus and began driving in a hurry. He was in such a hurry that he began driving rashly on the roads, he was so fast that he ran into a lorry laden with iron rods that slowed down to take a turn onto a road. The driver ran the bus as iron rods pierced into his stomach and chest; luckily he survived as medical help was close by. Many people in the bus were injured just because of one man's negligence.

Whenever we do training programmes, we make it a point to be at the destined spot half an hour in advance. In spite of all this caution we have a couple of our trainers failing to make it up. Any number of warning has not worked with these people. I would personally wake them up and request them to get ready, they would do it in my presence, but when I am not around or if I do not monitor it they land up late to the training hall. These people have made it a way-of-life. It is time we keep up our timing whether the others ask us or not.

The same case goes with landing up late, just because the saying 'better late than never' is told, that does not mean to say we have to turn up late and give a lame excuse that 'I have come late even though...'

I met a woman in one of my corporate programmes. She was around thirty three years of age, beautiful, well-mannered, educated and nice to speak to. I addressed her as 'Mrs' when she corrected me and said she was very much a spinster. I apologised to her and said 'I am sorry for my statement as I thought that you were married.'

Actually she looked like she was. When I enquired with her, she sadly said that her father was comparing her astrological chart with several men and it never matched. He was doing it for the last sixteen years. She endorsed her father's view as she was brought up in such a way.

One of her close relatives had married a boy whose horoscope had matched, the husband died in a fatal accident killing him on the spot. The girl was widowed at a young age of nineteen. She simply said, 'I will listen to what my father says, he knows what is right for me.' I advised her to marry at least now that she had time as it would be late if she waited any more. I simply told her 'better late than never'.

Most of us repent for not having done many things in life. Children ill-treat their parents and get ill-treated by their wards and realise why they are in such a position. They recall what they had done to their own parents who gave them everything in life. It is time that we realise and make the best of things and not repent later on.

We fail to do many things in life when we have to do it. We realise that it is too late; we repent for it and feel sad about it.

Recently I was in Bangalore for a weekend. I reside in Coimbatore to oversee the Tamilnadu operation of my company. While I was leaving both my parents came to the main gate to see me off. I touched the feet of my parents and sought their blessings. The auto-driver observed it.

While we were driving, he asked me, 'Sir, if you do not mind, can I ask you something?'

I just smiled and said, 'Go ahead.'

He asked, 'Were those your parents who came to see you off?'

I said, 'Yes, they are my parents.'

He then said, 'What a devotion, how lucky they are to get a son like you.'

I asked him, 'Why do you feel so? They are everything to me,' I said.

He was silent for a while and said, 'When my parents were alive, I ill-treated both of them and thought that they were a waste. Only now after they have gone, I realise how much they have done for me right from the day I was born.'

He says, 'I feel so sad because when they were in the evening of their lives, they did not get even three square meals.'

He wiped away the tears from his eyes and said, 'Oh, how foolish I was to have done that.'

He paused and said, 'I am sorry, sir, but I feel very guilty now.'

I consoled him and said 'Well you have done it unconsciously, anyway pray for their souls and now you could do a penance.'

He asked me, 'What is it and how can I compensate for that short-coming?'

I said, 'Trace out some aged relatives of yours and look after them as if they are your parents.'

He was happy and said 'I will do it right now after I drop you.'

He went on and said, 'I have my father's younger brother and his wife living. I will fall at their feet like the way you did and will look after them.'

I told him, 'That will bring you temporary joy and as such your uncle and aunt will also be very happy.'

While we reached the railway station, he held both my hands and said, 'You have turned a sinner into a good person.' He flatly refused to take the money. I had to force it into his hands. I was happy that I was in a position to help a person in life.

Let me give you seven examples of the same. They are:

1. A man had some small ailment, he ignored it. It later on turned into a big gland and diagnosed as cancer, he had to die. If only he had listened to advice, he would have survived.

2. A man went fishing in certain waters and was told that there were crocodiles. He dared the people and lost his limb.

3. There was a man who built a portion of his house and left it unfinished. His engineer cautioned him that it would collapse if it rains. He ignored the warning and the building fell down resulting in huge loss.

4. A woman who had a small ailment ignored it; she later realised that her disease had become incurable. She tried to save small money and landed up spending a huge sum for treatment.

5. A woman did not have a baby as she was afraid that she would lose her beauty. When she decided to go for a baby, she was tested and her blood had extra cholesterol and it was not advisable to have a baby. It was too late. The couple was forced to go without any issue.
6. My friend's father went on telling him to study hard as it would help him, but he ignored it. He went for an interview and realised how important education was. It was too late and he could do very little about it.
7. A drug addict was warned by the doctor to abstain from drugs. He went on till he realised that he had crossed the brim. He wanted to live normally like anyone, but it was too late. He was on the verge of dying.

In all the above cases you will find people are cautioned. They ignore advice and land up in trouble. If only one is cautious, he will not repent later. We have to do what we have to do it when it is required or else we will repent later.

A Soulful Story

While at the park one day, a woman sat down next to a man on a bench near a playground. 'That's my son over there,' she said, pointing to a little boy in a red sweater who was gliding down the slide.

'He's a fine looking boy' the man said. 'That's my son on the swing in the blue sweater.' Then, looking at his watch, he called to his son. 'What do you say we go, Todd?' Todd pleaded, 'Just five more minutes, Dad. Please? Just five more minutes.'

The man nodded and Todd continued to swing to his heart's content. Minutes passed and the father stood and called again to his son. 'Time to go now?' Again Todd pleaded, 'Five more minutes, Dad. Just five more minutes.' The man smiled and said, 'O.K.'

'You are certainly a patient father,' the woman responded.

The man smiled and then said, 'My older son Tommy was killed by a drunk driver last year while he was riding his bike near here. I never spent much time with Tommy and now I'd give anything for just five more minutes with him. I've vowed not to make the same mistake with Todd. He thinks he has five more minutes to swing. The truth is, I get five more minutes to watch him play.'

Life is all about making priorities, what are your priorities? Give someone you love 5 more minutes of your time today.

STORY

Jesus and Satan were having an on-going argument about who was better on the computer. They had been going at it for days, and frankly God was tired of hearing all the bickering.

Finally fed up, God said, 'That's it! I have had enough. I am going to set up a test that will run for two hours, and from those results, I will judge who does the better job.'

So Satan and Jesus sat down at the keyboards and typed away.
They moused.
They faxed.
They e-mailed.
They e-mailed with attachments.
They downloaded.
They did spreadsheets!
They wrote reports.
They created labels and cards.
They created charts and graphs.
They did some genealogy reports.
They did every job known to man.

Jesus worked with heavenly efficiency and Satan was faster than hell.

Then, ten minutes before their time was up, lightning suddenly flashed across the sky, thunder rolled, rain poured, and, of course, the power went off.

Satan stared at his blank screen and screamed every curse word known in the underworld.

Jesus just sighed.

Finally the electricity came back, and each of them restarted their computers. Satan started searching frantically, screaming:

It's gone! It's all gone! I lost everything when the power went out!'

Meanwhile, Jesus quietly started printing out all of his files from the past two hours of work.

Satan observed this and became irate.

'Wait!' He screamed. 'That's not fair! He cheated! How has he come all his work and I don't have any?'

God just shrugged and said,

Jesus saves!

Gloria and Pauline say that they don't wait for circumstances to change. Do something now. Don't wait for something or nothing to land in your lap, for your luck to turn, your ship to come in, for overnight success. Put those myths to rest and get on with your business. Don't wait for one big chance of a life time. Waiting is the major activity of that idea. Using opportunity is a business of one small chance at a time. At times we wait and wait and never do it, it is better we do it even though later than not doing it.

THE BEST IS YET TO BE

We may miss bus or may lose a match or even lose a good spouse and feel for it. God will give you a good one if He delays it as He has his own ways. Hope for the best.

◆◆◆

7

BE CAREFUL, ALWAYS

'*When you meet someone better than yourself, turn your thoughts to becoming his equal. When you meet someone not as good as you are, look within and examine yourself. When we seek to discover the best in others, We somehow bring out the best in ourselves.*'

Many people say that 'Whatever has to happen will happen and no one can stop that.'

This saying may be true to some extent, but what I state is when we can be careful, we have to be and must not just take things for granted. It is like a man who walks on the main road where traffic is busy, he says if I have to be run over by a vehicle no one can stop that. But if he is extra careful no harm can be done to him. Hence, we all must be careful and must not presume things and go by what is said about our own care.

We live in a very bad, dangerous and corrupt world where no one is safe unless and until we take measures to protect ourselves from external and internal dangers. Keeping this in mind we have to be very careful about where to tread, what to do and what not to do. The wrong action can lead us into trouble. At times we are our own enemy where we tend to make mistakes and realise it later on.

Threats can come from us, threats can also come from outside. At times when we are very casual, it comes from within. The same things can happen when we are cautious, it can come from outside. Threats are of three types.

They are:

1. Internal Threats
2. External Threats
3. Threats from nowhere.

Internal Threats: Many people are their own enemies. That is because they are not firm in their thinking and such wild thinking leads them into trouble. At times silly actions can also lead one into trouble.

Action to be taken – watch out! Ensure that your thoughts don't go wild. Refine your thinking and do good, all good will come out from your mind.

External Threats: Threats of this type is very common. We have people around who pretend that they are very friendly. We take them to be our friends, they turn foes just because of greed or at times to take revenge on us. We have to watch out for such external threats.

Action to be taken – watch out! Do not get carried away by people, evaluate a person even before you trust him or her, these days we do not know who is good and who is bad.

Threats From Nowhere: When we are very casual, we suddenly realise that our world is closing on us. Even before we think on how to act, the calamity comes and goes. We sit and brood over such calamities. At times it may happen to our own blabbering and utterances.

Action to be taken – watch out! When we know we live in a hostile country we have to gear up ourselves with ammunition. Similarly when we anticipate trouble we must be careful and remain prepared always.

As I told you my mother and older sister always caution me about keeping myself warm and having tablets for any emergency as I travel a lot. I ignore their advice and sometimes I pay very heavily for it. Once when I was leaving for Bangalore by an air-conditioned bus, I did not take my sweater along with me as I thought that Bangalore was also as hot as Coimbatore, where I was doing a project. I entered the bus and found that it was very cold, I remembered what my sister and mother had said, but I took their advice very casually.

I tried asking the bus driver to reduce the AC, he did, but soon a passenger went and told him that the AC was too low and he had no other go but to switch on the AC to its full extent. I suffered the whole night. To add to all this I found Bangalore very cold. I somehow managed to get a sweater from my brother. We must listen to advice from elders.

We have to be careful when we speak, when we decide and when we plan to do something. All said and done, we have to watch out whether we are speaking or we are making others speak. At times we buy a product without checking it, we presume that it is good and when we get home we find it is not working, we fret and fume, what were you doing when you had to check. Do it before you go further.

The incident I am about to tell you is really touching and real good one for all of us. The real contribution in life comes from the poor.

As the children were playing on the beach, a ragged woman was going around now and then picking something from the beach. Whenever she came across a child she would smile and greet the child. But the parents of the picnicking children told the children to keep away from the woman because she was dirty and poor.

Do you know what the old woman was doing? The old woman was picking up any broken glass on the beach so that the children wouldn't injure themselves.

In any society, the real contribution is made mostly by the poorer sections. They have a natural inclination to come to the rescue of the accident victims; the rich people in their cars will not bother even to look at the victims.

Daddy's Car in the Woods

Little Johnny watched his daddy's car pass by the school playground and go into the woods. Curious, he followed the car and saw daddy and aunt Jane in a passionate embrace.

Little Johnny found this so exciting that he could hardly contain himself as he ran home and started to tell his mother. 'Mummy, I was at the playground and I saw daddy's car go into the woods with aunt Jane. I went back to look and he was giving aunt Jane a big kiss, and then he helped her take off her shirt. Then aunt Jane helped daddy take off his pants, then aunt Jane.'

At this point mummy cut him off and said, 'Johnny, this is such an interesting story, suppose you save the rest of it for supper time. I want to see the look on daddy's face when you tell it tonight.'

At the dinner table that evening, mummy asked little Johnny to tell his story. Johnny started his story, 'I was at the playground and I saw daddy's car go into the woods with aunt Jane. I went back to look and he was giving aunt Jane a big kiss, then he helped her take off her shirt. Then aunt Jane helped daddy take his pants off, then aunt Jane and daddy started doing the same thing that mummy and uncle Bill used to do when daddy was in the army.'

Mummy fainted.

Moral: Sometimes you need to listen to the whole story before you interrupt!

Telling Lies

One day Kuttappan's dad bought a robot.

The robot was special in that it could detect a lie and would slap the person who lied on the face.

Kuttappan returned late from school that day and his dad asked him, 'Son, why are you late from school?'

Kuttappan answered, 'Dad we had extra classes today.'

Much to his astonishment the robot jumped up and slapped Kuttappan on his face.

His dad told him, 'Mone (son) this robot is special in that he can detect a lie and will then slap the person who lied now come on tell me the truth, why are you late?'

'Dad I went for a movie', 'which movie?' 'The Ten Commandments', S-p-la-tt Kuttappan got a tight slap on the face from the robot.

'Sorry dad...I lied again, honestly I went for an adult movie.'

Dad: 'Shame on you son when I was your age I never used to do such shameful things.'

Splatt, the dad gets a tight slap on the face from the robot.

Hearing all this, Kuttappan's mother comes walking out of the kitchen saying, 'Athu pinne enginnenaa, ningalude monealle?' (After all he is your son, he will be like you), to which the robot steps up and gives a resounding slap on Kuttappan's mother's face.

THOUGHT

The Best Things to Give

To your Creator - is devotion
To your Father - is humility
To your Mother - is good conduct
To your Teacher - is obedience
To your Friend - is sincerity
To your Opponent - is tolerance
To yourself - is respect
To your Enemy - is forgiveness
To all Men - is charity

STORY

One must be cautious as to what he wants. Once upon a time, there was a poor old man who carried heavy sticks from one place to another for his survival. One day, as he was on his way with the heavy load on his back, he grew very tired and hence sat on the bank of a nearby river and said – 'I am so sick and tired of this; I only wish that death would come and relieve me.'

Instantly, Death slipped up and said – 'Here I am, what you want me to do?' The old man was astonished beyond words.

The old man said – 'I want you to put this bundle of sticks on my back again.'

Two things can be derived from this story. One is that no one is interested to die, unless they commit suicide at the spur of the moment. No one would commit suicide with elaborate planning. Suicide is a very spontaneous decision which one takes without thinking about the repercussions. The second is, that whatever we wish for would come to fruition. Therefore, we must be careful about what we wish for. We must also choose our wishes very carefully.

One must be careful, not just careful but extra-careful in whatever he does. There must be concentration in what one does and one must also do things with devotion or else things may go haywire and at times we may land up in trouble. That is why I say we must be careful in whatever we do. We must be extra-careful when we drive a vehicle, when we walk on the road or when we are doing something with fire.

THE BEST IS YET TO BE

We must always be careful, at times danger can be as close as possible and yet not attack us, but at times it will come and attack us. Remember that good times will always come. Hope for the best.

◆◆◆

8

TOUGH TIMES NEVER LAST, GOOD TIMES REMAIN

Unless we have a combination of both the tough as well as the good times, there is no fun. In fact tough times are what make us learn lessons to get through turbulent times. Tough times will come and go, but be sure good times will remain forever.

Somehow we do not understand or even know why we face problems and have tough times. Is it because of our own folly or is it because things are pre-destined? Or is it because of our previous sins, or is it because of certain circumstances that come our way? No one is in a position to explain anything about this. But still I must state that we can and must face tough times and must never run away from it. When we face tough times and tide over that period and we begin to do well in life, we sit back and think, we tell it to the others and take pride in sharing how we struggled which itself indicates that there is a certain reason why we have tough times. May be to toughen us and show us what suffering is all about.

Man frets and fumes over his problems and sometimes

even ends his life. One must understand three important things. Firstly, sufferings are a part and parcel of life without which we will not lead a meaningful life. The second is, we can overcome sufferings by managining them rather than weeping over. The third factor is suffering will always not be with us, they will leave us, they are like visitors who will come and go away. If we treat visitors well they will want to stay for a longer time and if we look after them and say, 'Look it's time you should leave,' they will leave gloriously. If we understand these facts then we will have a good life.

Every man on this earth is faced with some problem or the other. It depends on the degree of sufferings we have so also how we take it when we get it. If we take it casually it will leave us soon. If we cling to it and go very deep into it, it will tend to remain with us. For some, suffering is a part and parcel of life. But if we use the God given senses that we have been endowed with, we can overcome it. Unfortunately many people feel that sufferings and tough times are something pre-destined and we have to live with them and that is why we suffer so much.

God created man with an intention to give him a good life. Man was to obey God, but he fell for Satan's pranks. In spite of the warning by God that the devil was lurking around, man never listened to God. What the original man did was called a sin. He disobeyed God and till date we are facing the same problem and the world is divided among the good and the evil.

We have seen three parts of the world where evil and good were divided. They are:

1. The Good Old World
2. The Previous World
3. The World Today.

The Good Old World: Good - 80% Evil - 20%

The Previous World: Good - 50% Evil - 50%

The World Today: Good - 20% Evil - 80%

I must state that the previous world that existed during the time of our ancesors was a beautiful and better world than what we live in today. Yes, of course they did not have modern cars, latest gadgets and the comforts that we have today, but they surely had more of natural resources, corruption free world, pollution free world and better standards of living. In those days to bring up six children was an easy task, but today to bring up one child parents have to run around from pillar to post.

I still remember my father would pay one hundred and twenty five rupees as annual fees for our school. But today my son is just four-year-old, we have to cough up nearly a lakh as his fees. This is what the world is today – commercial, corrupt and competitive.

Things are taking a bad shape and hence the suffering of man has also increased. God is not to be blamed as it is man who does all the evil and then blames God for it. A man went and asked God why there was so much evil in the world today. God replied it was man who was responsible for doing it and not God. God warns man of certain things and yet man does it and falls in the pit that he digs for someone else.

I can assure you of one thing and that is tough times will never last forever, but they will go away. What is more important is what we have learnt when we have faced tough times. I have seen people have come out like gold after they have faced tough times. I have also come across people who have become rude, arrogant and inaccessible after they have faced tough times.

I personally have faced tough times. I have come out like gold. I now know what to do and what not to do. Most importantly I have learnt my lessons. I have seen what hardship is and who people are. People are like rats that desert a ship when it is sinking. They will not stand by you in your times of difficulty. I have also learnt one thing and that is when you are penniless no one will want to stay with you, befriend you or want to support you. They will discard you.

But if I look at my past, that is the time when I had sunshine in my life. I was just the opposite. I have stood by my friends and relatives when they are in difficult days. I have supported people in distress. I gave my friends room to stay when they had none. I helped friends financially, I helped people in many ways without even realising what would be in store for me. But one day when I fell and I was in darkness not a single person came to my rescue. I had done my best and had shown the world that I can be different when it came to supporting those who are in distress.

James Allen says, 'When you are in troubled times, lift up your thoughts and thereby lift up your life.' A man will find that as he alters his thoughts towards things and other people, things, and other people will alter towards him. Let a man radically alter his thoughts, and he will be astonished at the rapid transformation it will effect in the material conditions of his life. A man can only remain weak and abject and miserable by refusing to lift up his thoughts.

Accept everything with joy. In life we are used to getting bouquets and brickbats. At times we will get more bricks than bouquets but there are also occasions where we will get more bouquets than brickbats. We have to accept all this as times will change.

Difficulties will haunt you like an evil spirit if your time is really bad. It is during this time that you must not quit when you meet with failure. One of the most common causes of failure is the habit of quitting when one is overtaken by temporary defeat. Every person is guilty of this mistake at one time or another.

It is during this time that worries will plague you and discouragement will pour into your life like water flowing from a dam. But you must believe that all things are good for you. It is during this time that no one can lift you but you yourself alone. Think not for today but keep in mind that there is a million tomorrows. If you fail today, surely there is a good tomorrow.

You have to bear the trials and annoyances of life will bring about patience. Do not take any drastic step and come to a conclusion about troubles as they will come to pass. Every great man except those who have taken the mantle from their parents will tell you how they built up their empires that are doing well today. Very few men have come up without struggle in life. In every trial and trouble you will learn lessons.

When you have tough times, put up with them and wait for good times to come. Remember if a man has less tough times and more good times that means he has been in a position to fight himself out of the tough times. But if man challenges times and he challenges God, he will suffer and not God. Hence it is better to face difficulties when you are young and full of energy and hope rather than suffer at an old age where no one will ever be willing to take you with them or even help you.

THOUGHT

Abraham Lincoln says:
'Are you bound to win and succeed all the time?
I am bound to win, but I am bound to be true.
I am not bound to succeed, but I am bound to live up to the light I have.
I must stand with anybody that stands right, stand with him while he is right,
and part with him when he goes wrong.'

STORY

Once a farmer had a horse which he used to plough fields and it ran away one day. The neighbours came to console the farmer. He said that it was good as his horse came with another horse along with it.

The neighbours admired the farmer and said 'how lucky you are,' for which the farmer replied.

I am not lucky, my son tried riding the horse and he broke his arm.

The neighbour said that it was terrible.

The farmer said he was lucky as authorities came to recruit young men for war, they went away.

My son managed to stay back and developed the land; he is married and built a house.

Our problems are also a blessing in disguise. Hence whatever happens to us is for our own good, we have to face it.

THE BEST IS YET TO BE

Tough times never last, but good times always remain. After a long battle and great struggle we will one day sit back and realise that our struggle was fun and that we wish we get it back. Hope for the best.

♦♦♦

9

CHARITY – A GREAT DEED

With malice toward none; with charity for all. And now abideth faith, hope, charity, these three, but the greatest of these is charity. Verily I say unto you. Inasmuch as ye have done it unto one of the least of these my brethren, ye have done it unto me.

The concept of a trust or a charitable organisation was simply to serve the poor. An organisation with like minded people with a philanthropic mind would join hands and start a charitable trust to serve the under-privileged. But today the very concept has been redefined with successful companies and individuals starting a trust to make money in the name of charity. These people do not realise that they are sucking the blood of the poor for no man or company which makes money in the name of the poor shall thrive.

The world has got two types of people. They are:

1. The 'haves' and
2. The 'have-nots'.

The haves: These are the people who have everything at their disposal. Most of them inherit property and money from their ancestors. But many people do not feel like giving as they feel that if they give they will also fall into the category of the have-nots.

The have-nots: These are the people who are born poor and do not have anything with them. They try to make an earning and rarely succeed. They depend on the haves who exploit them. Till date we have not heard of a man writing his property in the names of his servant or people who worked for them.

The first thing that the haves want is to have a successor, preferably a son to carry forward their mission (of exploiting and denying the poor of their rights).

The 'haves' are required to help the 'have-nots.' But we have people who rob the have-nots directly or indirectly. The haves rob the have-nots directly by extracting work and paying a pittance. They also rob the have-nots by getting money in the name of charity and living in luxury.

The Thirukkural says: 'Share your food with the hungry and help life in all forms. Refrain from causing death to any form of life. All the codes endorse this. Life is dear, but even to save your life, do not do that which will deprive another creature of its own dear life.'

God gives you a lot of things, but if you don't return something to the world, then there is no use of the goodness that we have received from God. We all must understand that all of us have not got the gift of richness, only a few of us have got it. Hence I feel we must and should do some good in terms of charity.

I do charity once in a way. One of my close friends who is very stingy by nature discourages me saying that we are pampering the poor by giving them help. They tend to get lazy and do not want to work hard for their livelihood but they get easy money from us. I agreed to what he said to certain extent, but I too believe that we must do charity but for the disabled ones and not for those who are hale and hearty. He also argued, 'Why should we give our hard earned money to someone when it belongs to us?'

I asked him a poser, 'Do you not look after your parents, siblings and children? What have they done for you?' He was silent and after a while retorted, 'After all they are our relatives, another thing is when we are in trouble, they will help us.' I told him yes, they will help us when we are in trouble. At the same time we will get help from God through some source.

At this juncture it is worth mentioning the name of JRD Tata, a great Indian philanthropist and one of the pioneers of the industry in India. He was a great man who earned through fair means and distributed money to the needy. His charity was something that we people remember even today. That is the reason why God gave him a long and blissful life.

There is also another businessman who lived during our time. He was very unfair in his dealings. He never did any business without fraud. He never did any charity and died early. It is also worth mentioning the name of 'Bill Gates' who relinquished his office just to take up charity for the underprivileged. We have to learn lessons from such great people.

Even Andrew Carnegie the great steel magnate said, 'I will work for the first half and earn money and the second half I will give away what I got in the first half.'

I would like to compare charity to the animal kingdom where you have different types of animals. Some are dominant and rule over the others. The smaller ones are at the mercy of the bigger ones. One may have heard about a lion or a tiger hunting down a deer, buffalo or a zebra, but you would not have heard about a couple of deer trying to attack a lion. That is the way in which God has created the animal world.

The best example of charity is Mother Teresa of the Missionaries of Charity. She was a true and living example of what charity was. She took care of the poor, needy, destitutes and old and dying people. Such people were rejected by their own people and had no place to go. This is where Mother played an important role.

She looked after people unmindful of caste, creed, gender and religion. She only looked at the human suffering in a person. She loved people so much that she gave her entire life working in very dirty and difficult conditions taking care of the sick, needy and unwanted in society. Today Mother has made history, but the work that she did, was appreciated by people from all over the world.

Another typical example is the living sage Satya Sai Baba of Puttaparthi. For some he is God, for many he is a saint, for millions he is a re-incarnation of some great saint. All the more, he is wonderful saint who has a great following, all his followers are true believers in him and his philosophy. He gets several crores of rupees as donations. He never retains anything for himself. He gives it all to the poor and the needy. Great political leaders from India and the world come and prostrate before this living legend.

God had created man into different categories. The three categories are:

1. Able
2. Unable
3. Disabled

Able: This category of people attract wealth. They have money and power at their disposal and can buy anything and do anything they want. Even people in society respect this category and are afraid of them in a sense.

Unable: This category can only work for the first group. They are basically people who can execute what is told. They cannot think and depend on the thinking power of the first category.

Disabled: This category of people cannot do anything. They are the ones who need charity. There are also people in this category who take advantage and laze away at the cost of others. We have to identify such lazy people. In the bargain the actually disabled ones must not suffer.

Most often the second and third category of people are dependent on the first category.

There is another important thing to remember. If a man who has a lot of wealth gives it away to the ones who do not possess it, he will have nothing for himself and he may also fall into the category of the have-nots. And for that matter if wealth falls into the wrong hands, it is likely to be squandered, that is people who have not seen wealth may not know how to manage it.

That reminds me of a parable in the Bible. A rich man came to Jesus and asked what he must do to get peace. Jesus told him, 'Go and sell all your wealth and give it to the poor and you will get peace.' The man was shocked and never expected Jesus to tell him such a thing. He just bowed down and walked away as to indicate that he was not in favour of what Jesus had said. Jesus at this juncture commented, 'It is easier for a camel to go through the eye of a needle than a rich man to give away all his wealth.'

While doing charity, remember certain things. We must do charity only if we have the resources with us. Secondly we must identify and trace out people who are actually needy and help them. Whatever we do will come to us in a bigger and better form.

STORY

There was once a school teacher who taught Moral Science to the students. Once, she instructed her students to go out and be good. One of the students went out after school hours and walked down the streets, distributing gifts to the poor and helping whoever needed help.

The next day he told the teacher of his good deed. But the teacher was not impressed by his action.

She said that she wanted him to be good and not to do things to show off. There is a great difference between the two which only a few understand.

We have seen many instances that people offer gifts and other material goods to the poor and downtrodden without being good. Such actions of charity are done mainly for publicity and not with the genuine intention to help others. Goodness stems from good thoughts and intentions.

THE BEST IS YET TO BE

Charity is a great deed. There are people who do charity even when they are down and out. They do it with joy; such people will get back in multiples soon. Whatever may be your position learn to do charity. Hope for the best.

◆◆◆

10

HOPE AGAINST HOPE

Hope is something that is given to mankind. Most often it is hidden. It comes only after a long wait for some, but it does not come for many people who die a miserable death. But those who have hope in themselves will surely get what they want.

One thing which we all live with is hope. We should always hope for the best things to come. A old widow in Russia who sent her son to war to an enemy country waited for thirteen years to see her son return. Many people had told her that her son was dead and buried in the enemy country, but she refused to believe in what they said. She welcomed every soldier who came from war and enquired from them about her son. So great was her hope that she believed that her only son would return.

Same is the case with human beings who do many things with hope. Take for example when there is a vacancy in a company where there is just one vacancy and ten people attend the interview. One thing common in all these people is that all have hope that they will get the job. Eventually only one person will get the job, but the nine out of the ten will live on hope. They will come to know that their hope is dashed only when the results are announced.

The same nine people who lose out in this interview will not hesitate to go on attending interviews till they get a job. A very good friend of mine borrowed some money from me. When I needed that money I went on frequenting his house to get it back. There came a day when I found the door locked. When I enquired with the landlord, he said they had vacated the house as they were unable to pay the rent. My hopes were dashed, but I kept visiting his house with the hope that I would get the money back. I saw his wife one day at Church, she pretended as if she had not seen me and walked away. I then realised that they were not interested in returning my money and finally lost hope and gave it up. God has given me several times that amount because of my faith in the creator.

I came across a Colonel who told me this real life incident about his old mother who was taken to the command hospital in Bangalore. She was very sick and was in her death-bed. The doctor checked her thoroughly at her behest and asked her what her last wish was. The woman remained silent. The Colonel and the doctor waited patiently as they thought that she would ask for some favourite dish or ask for some relative. But they were shocked when she said what her last wish. She said loudly, 'I am not happy with you doctor; I have hope that I will live.'

She looked at her son and said, 'Well son if you really love mama, I want to see another doctor.'

Sometimes we find wealthy people going in for a heart operation knowing pretty well that the operation won't help. I met a family friend of mine who is a heart surgeon.

One day as we were discussing he said, 'Look the heart is such a sensitive organ that if we even touch it with our hands, it tends to get damaged. Imagine we people cut it open, rip it, stitch it and even try to make it function.'

I asked him why you would go for an open heart surgery when you knew about this fact. He said, 'Simple, people have hopes that they will live, and that is why we do it.' People get operated with a hope that they will live again. We all live on hopes in life and do not want to give up.

Some of the hopes that we have are:

1. *Losing a Job:* When we lose a job, we are hopeful that we will get another one.
2. *Losing a match:* When we lose a match or a race, we are hopeful that we will win a race someday.
3. *Showing the Door:* When we are shown the door at a meeting or a place where go to seek help, we still have hope we will be entertained.
4. *Incurable Disease:* When the doctor says that our disease is not curable, we still have some hope in our heart that the God above will save us.
5. *An Athlete:* When an athlete runs a race and loses, he attempts again with the hope that he will win.
6. *Election Contest:* A man who contests an election, loses and tries again as he has hopes that the second time people would vote in his favour.
7. *Everything is Lost:* When we lose everything in life, including our spouse or a dear one, we still live on hopes that God will be kind to us.

If I take my own example, sometime back I was in a very bad shape. I had no money to even pay my rent. My landlord who was a very kind person tolerated me. There was a small grocery shop who gave me things on credit. My mother supported me with food and some money. I lived like this for more than three years. During this time I continued writing my books. I always had a hope that I would shine in life. I must give that credit to my beloved father who once said, 'You are a very intelligent boy, you are above the rest, the only difference is you do not have money, but one day you will shine and the rest of the world will look upon you as a hero.' These words lent an encouraging stance in my life. I still keep recalling it. This is where I had hope in myself and my abilities.

I am basically a person who depends largely on research, surveys and statistics where any aspect is concerned. On one occasion when I was doing a project for my management course, I went around to several shops and met people who used soaps to get the exact information about the usage and sales of soaps. There were many of my colleagues who did nothing but collected facts from old books and just put some facts together to make the project look like a good one. Mine also was the same type, the only difference is that I worked hard for it.

Similarly I have given facts in this book which I worked hard on. There are no facts taken from sources, except some thoughts and stories. That brings me to the subject on hope. I met a man on the streets who was stranded in life. I asked him, 'Do you know where you are heading?' He smiled, paused and said, 'I have hope that fate will shine on me someday.'

Same is the case with a friend of mine who was our senior in school. He has a lot of vague ideas which were not accepted by anybody. He is unmarried and is still waiting for the girl in his life. When I asked him to go search for one, he says, 'The girl who is destined to marry me will come one day.' He has a lot of hopes in life.

That is the greatness of hope in life. We all live on the hope that we will have what we want, at times when we lose everything we still have one great possession, that is hope. Hope does a lot for man in life. If hope is lost everything is lost. Hence we have to always have hope in life. We must accept finite disappointments. But we must never lose infinite hope.

STORY

A poor lady who worked in a stone quarry had an only son. She was not in a position to give him care as she was engrossed in her work. The only time that she gave her son was late in the evening when she returned home. Even at that time the boy would be sleeping. It was a routine life for her as she was forced to work to save her and her only son.

Her husband was working in the quarry and was run over by a lorry which was reversing. The careless lorry driver was reversing at a great speed without looking at the back. This man was run over and died immediately. The owner of the quarry did not compensate the family with money; all he did was to take care of the funeral expenses and gave the widow a small sum. When she began badgering him for money, he said that she could work in the quarry in her husband's place which she did.

One day when this lady had left her son under a tree, he was bitten by a poisonous snake and died instantly. The workers realised it very late. In her grief she carried the dead child to all her neighbours, asking them for medicine, and the people said, 'She has lost her senses. The boy is dead.'

At last this lady met a man who replied to her request, 'I cannot give you medicine for your child, but I know a physician who can. The woman said, 'Pray tell me, sir, who is it?' and the man replied, 'Go to Shakyamuni, the Buddha.'

She then approached the Buddha with all hope and confidence and cried, 'Lord and Master, give me the medicine that will make my boy come to life.'

The Buddha promised to help her provided she would bring a handful of mustard seed. The woman was extremely happy at this condition and was hastening to procure what he wanted. But the Buddha added a rider. She agreed.

Shakyamnni Buddha said, 'The mustard seed must be taken

from a house where no one has lost a child, husband, parent or friend.' The lady went from house to house, and the people pitied her and said, 'Here is mustard seed; take it!' But when she asked, 'Did a son or daughter, a father or mother, die in your family?' They answered her, 'Alas! The living is few, but the dead are many. Do not remind us of our deepest grief.' And there was no house but some beloved one had died in it.

To the desolate woman the realization came that, like a lamp, the lives of men flicker up and were extinguished again. At last the darkness of the night reigned everywhere. And she considered the fate of men that thought to herself, 'How selfish I am in my grief! Death is common to all; yet in the valley of desolation there is a path that leads him to immortality, who has surrendered all selfishness.'

THE BEST IS YET TO BE

Tough times never last, but good times always remain. After a long battle and great struggle we will one day sit back and realise that our struggle was fun and that we wish we get it back. Hope for the best.

◆◆◆

11

BE DEAF, AT TIMES

It is better to be deaf at times when vague comments are made against us. We can decide to reply politely to what is said, that is if it is actually required. The best defence is to keep quiet when such a comment is made.

When I say we have to 'be deaf at times,' What I mean to say is that one has to be deaf to bad things and comments that may mar your growth in life. Day in and day out we come across comments against us. If we take them seriously, we will do more of fire-fighting than looking out at our own future. Some of us are in the habit of reacting very fast to such comments. That is not advisable. If we keep answering or giving back at every comment that comes to us, we will exhaust our energies and may not be in a position to do anything constructive at all.

You must also remember people abuse us for two reasons; one is because they are upset and angry with us and the other reason is that they are interested in our welfare and are actually checking us. It depends on how we take it. When I showed my first book to some of my close friends many people appreciated what I had done. But there were also many people who termed my book as 'rubbish.' I did not take their words seriously as I would not have been writing my seventh book now. I was deaf to their comments.

I still remember the comments made by my late Principal when I was a student.

He said, 'You will not prosper in life, I am sure you will land up as an ordinary worker or a porter in a railway station.'

He was trying to tell me I would do badly in life. He continued to snub me day in and day out for reasons best known to him. One day he disgraced me in front of all the students which put me off very badly. That whole night I was upset and did not sleep. I consulted a teacher who was very close to me. She was never married and treated me like her own son and said, 'If you take our Principal seriously, I have something different to tell you and that is, 'You are poised to do very well and will shine in life, success will haunt you like an evil spirit, take my words it will come true.'

I began weeping profusely. She consoled me and encouraged me and said, 'You are a courageous boy, I do not expect you to cry like this, let this be the last time, take it from me, you will shine in life and I stand by what I say.'

Her soothing words consoled me to a large extent. I was relieved at what she said. This is where I learnt to discard the negative comments that were made against me. There were a lot of students who took the comments of parents and elders to their hearts and have suffered to a great extent. Even today many of them suffer and blame the elders for what they are today.

One day when one of our teachers asked us our ambition in life, many students came out with great ideas.

My turn was about to come when I recalled what my Principal has said, 'You could choose from being a coolie, a servant or a cart-puller.'

I gathered courage and said, 'I want to become a great person.'

All the students laughed at me. My teacher smiled and just kept that in mind. The same school invited me as a guest of honour and said, 'The one and only trainer and author of several books is here.'

My Principal was not there at that time he had passed away.

Fortunately I did not take his comments seriously. Some of the students took his and our teachers' comments very seriously and lived with it. One day when I went to the place where I did my schooling, I met an old friend of mine who is on a hand-to-mouth basis said that he was not doing too well in life. He said he was trying out everything possible, but nothing seemed to work, he had a feeling that it might be the curses that he got from his parents, neighbours, relatives and teachers that had brought him to that state. I tried speaking to him, but that thing was deeply embedded in his mind which could not be phased out.

Some years later when I went to see my teachers at Hubli, I made it a point to see my teacher who had motivated me. She was happy to see me settled in life and driving my own car. We had a lengthy discussion in which I told her about my work. We also discussed about what my late Principal had told me. We made it a point to visit his grave and pray there for a while.

My teacher commented, 'The way in which you have not kept what he had said and visited his grave itself indicates your big heart', she then said, 'God will bless you with more success.'

When I wrote my first book, I took the manuscript to my maternal uncle and showed it to him with an intention of getting some financial help.

He never even took it from my hand; he asked me, 'What it was?'

I said, 'I was planning to write a book.'

He discouraged me and said that we do not come from the family of writers and are not related to Shakespeare or George Bernard Shaw. He simply asked me to get a job and earn a living. I was disappointed, but took it up as a challenge. I wrote the book and took it to show him.

He commented, 'After all you are my nephew and you have proved it.'

I was deaf to his negative comments.

This the seventh book of mine that you are reading.

Hence I state that one must be deaf to vague comments that come to us. Take it positively and tell yourself that you will and can prove this person wrong, at the same time do not try to take revenge or tell people that you have overcome such a problem. That stands understood; you don't have to convince anybody about anything when they say you will not do well and now that you are doing well.

At times, what people say, may instigate you to do something just to prove them wrong, in the bargain you will stand to gain.

There was once a boy, who was dismissed and sent back from the school because his teachers claimed that he was too stupid to learn anything. He came back and told his disheartened mom. She told him to ignore their comments. She came forward to teach him. This boy didn't go to any school or university and was self-taught. Years later the same boy grew up to create history in the scientific world.

The boy's name is Thomas Alva Edison. It is pathetic that some teachers make unholy remarks on the students which may lead to discouragement and make them discontinue the school itself. In respect of Edison his mother came forward and encouraged him. But for the encouragement of his mother the world would have lost a super genius in the scientific world. This is a lesson to all the parents.

THOUGHT

Pope John Paul says:

'You must have the courage to accept life as it is. This means loving one's times, without vain regrets and without mythical utopias, convinced that each one has a mission to carry out, that life is a gift received and must be bestowed on others, whether the times are serene or intricate, peaceful or troubled, but it is not enough to accept life as it is. It is necessary to transform life from a self-centred to a other centred position.'

Frog Leap

Once upon a time there was a bunch of tiny frogs .... Who arranged a running competition.

The goal was to reach the top of a very high tower.

A big crowd had gathered around the tower to see the race and cheer on the contestants....

The race began....

Honestly, no one in the crowd really believed that the tiny frogs would reach the top of the tower.

You heard statements such as:

'Oh, way too difficult!'

'They will never make it to the top.'

or:

'Not a chance that they will succeed. The tower is too high!' The tiny frogs began collapsing. One by one.... Except for those, who in a fresh tempo, were climbing higher and higher....

The crowd continued to yell, 'It is too difficult! No one will make it!' More tiny frogs got tired and gave up.... But one continued higher and higher and higher.... This one wouldn't give up!

At the end everyone else had given up climbing the tower.

Except for the one tiny frog who, after a big effort, was the only one who reached the top!

Then all of the other tiny frogs naturally wanted to know how this one frog managed to do it?

A contestant asked the tiny frog how he had found the strength to succeed and reach the goal.

It turned out....

That the winner was DEAF! The moral of this story is: Never listen to other people's tendencies to be negative or pessimistic.... Because they take your most wonderful dreams and wishes away from you - the ones you have in your heart! Always think of the power, words have.

Be positive, be deaf when people tell you that you cannot do it.

Where humour is concerned, what you use in the whole of your life is nothing compared to what is yet to be, hence keep increasing it and make life a pleasure to live in. Laugh, be merry and make others happy. If you are not laughing, begin today; if you are already laughing top it up right now.

THE BEST IS YET TO BE

We have to be deaf to certain negative comments and suggestions. There are great personalities today who were snubbed by their parents for wasting time. Today they have a great following. We have to wait for the best to come. Hope for the best.

◆◆◆

12

GRACE BEFORE MEALS

There are many people who do not have even one square meal. When we get three meals or even one meal we have to thank God for that gift as it is something which we all human beings need. Food is a gift of God and that gift must be reciprocated by a small prayer to God.

In this world to get three square meals is a big wonder for several people. To get even one square meal is a matter of great effort to many. I have known and seen people starving to death. The ones who have food either waste it or do not know its value. The person who wastes his food will realise its value only when he/she does not get enough food to eat. Hence it is neceassry that we respect and don't waste food. We must also learn to give what we have to those who do not have food. Unfortunately it is pretty difficult for us to realise who is in need of food and who is not.

Sometime ago we had a prayer meeting at my mother's place. My parents are in the habit of feeding the poor during the time of Mother Mary's festival. I was in Bangalore and I took the food along with my cousin to a temple where there were many beggars.

We began distributing food when a beggar asked me, 'Is this vegetarian or non-vegetarian food? I told him, 'Well this is mutton biriyani and chicken kababs.'

Immediately his face brightened.

He then said, 'Today is Sunday and you see I am fond of non-vegetarian food.'

I simply distributed the food and walked away towards the car.

As we were driving home my cousin a little confused asked me out of curiosity, 'Is that really non-vegetarian food?'

I said, 'No, it is plain dhal rice, some masala rice and one side-dish.'

We both had a hearty laugh.

My cousin commented, 'How arrogant beggars can be today!'

I still remember as a child I got a sound thrashing from my father for starting my dinner without praying. At that moment I was angry with my father. For that moment I was angry with God too as He was the cause for my beating. I then took to praying to God in a negative way. One day we had a retreat where a priest and a nun handled our sessions. One of the topics was about food, its importance and why we must pray and thank God for it.

The priest said that we must be thankful to God as he gives us the food as a gift to us. Many people in the world are denied of food. There are several millions who die of hunger. When we get a meal, it is a gift from God; hence we have to thank him. During these sessions we had to sit and listen to all that the priest said.

In the end he asked us, 'My dear children, do you have any questions to ask me?'

I raised my hand and said I had a question, but that was a very personal one.

The priest asked me, 'What is it regarding?'

I said, 'That it was regarding food and prayer.'

He said there was nothing personal about it. I opened up and told him how I prayed angrily to God. He smiled and gave me a beautiful suggestion that whatever happens with God is good for us. God must not be blamed. I thought about it for a while and came to a conclusion; why blame God for the beating my dad had given me?

It was lunch time and we all gathered at the dining hall for lunch. The table was spread out with simple but good dishes for us. We had varieties of all food. As usual we had to begin our lunch with a prayer. Usually the main priest sits in a particular chair and leads the prayer. That day I was in for a shock when I was asked to occupy the chair and lead the prayer. I was emotional, nevertheless happy that I was asked to lead the prayer. I did that with great devotion. All of them followed me. After the prayer the main priest thanked me and asked me what I felt about the short conversation with God.

I simply said, 'God was not angry with me', and he smiled.

From that day onwards till today, I pray and I am happy with God and more so with my father who taught me a beautiful lesson. Today when I sit to dine with my dad, I feel it is a great opportunity as I rarely get to stay with him. I thank him and also thank God. I have also deleted the anger on my dad from my mind who did it for my own good. God is great, my father is even greater than me among human beings on this earth, and another great person is my mother who served food for me from my childhood. Even today I take chances to eat with them as I feel privileged.

It is important that we pray specially for our benefactors who are responsible for our food. It may be our parents, siblings, relatives, spouses, in-laws or even neighbours. It is important that we thank these people who give us our food as man has one important thing in life and that is to get his stomach full and there cannot be a great joy like food as no man has ever survived without food.

One of the reasons why we have to pray to God is because he is kind enough to give us our daily bread. If you look at the world today, there are many people who cannot afford even one single meal a day and hence when we get a meal, we must be happy to have it and hence thank God whom we believe blesses us with food.

There is a story of an arrogant millionaire who had tons of money and invited the wrath of several people in his vicinity. There came a day when he could not use all his money on the earth to get food. No one was willing to give him food. He was once told by a holy man to pray before he eats.

He simply said, 'Why should we thank God? We do not know where He is and I have the money and I don't see the need to thank Him. My power and money gives me the food and not God.'

I have been brought up with saying prayers every now and then. I have the habit of praying at the drop of a hat. This habit is embedded in me so deep that I can afford to forget anything, but not my prayers. Whenever I begin to eat I pray for three things. They are:

1. For God, thanking Him for the beautiful meal He has given me. (I know several people do not have one square meal a day.)

2. For my benefactors who have made it possible for me to have my food.

3. Again! To God for blessing the food, so that it becomes positive energy and that it may not cause any complication for me.

Grace at a Restaurant

Once a man took his children to a restaurant. His six-year-old son asked if he could say grace. As we bowed our heads he said, 'God is good, God is great. Thank you for the food, and I would even thank you more if mom gets us ice cream for dessert. And for liberty and justice for all, Amen!'

Along with the laughter from the other customers nearby, he heard a woman remark, 'That's what's wrong with this country. Kids today don't even know how to pray. Asking God for ice cream. Why, I never!'

Hearing this, the son burst into tears and asked his father, 'Did I do it wrong? Is God mad at me?'

The father held him and assured him that he had done a terrific job, and that God was certainly not mad at him, an elderly gentleman approached the table. He winked at the son and said, 'I happen to know that God thought that was a great prayer.' 'Really?' the son asked, 'Cross my heart,' the man replied. Then, in a theatrical whisper, he added (indicating the woman whose remark had started this whole thing), 'Too bad she never asks God for ice cream. A little ice cream is good for the soul sometimes.'

Naturally, the man bought his kids ice cream at the end of the meal. The son stared at his for a moment, and then did something which anyone will remember for the rest of their life. He picked up his sundae and, without a word, walked over and placed it in front of the woman. With a big smile he told her, 'Here, this is for you. Ice cream is good for the soul sometimes; and my soul is good already.'

Moments:

1. Happy moments - praise God.
2. Difficult moments - seek God.
3. Quiet moments - worship God.
4. Painful moments - trust God.
5. Every moment - thank God.

Guru Nanak says:
Prayer does not constitute words but virtues.
The first is truth.
The second is righteousness.
The third is charity.
The fourth is pure aspiration.
The fifth is praise and glory of God.
And let deeds of service be thy creed.

I would like to sum up this chapter with a beautiful example. Once a rich man was put in a closed room and not given anything for one full day. He went to bed hungry. That night God appeared to him and asked him what were his three wishes. God gave him three options..

The three wishes were:

1. A Diamond Mine
2. A Million Dollars
3. Food

The man said, 'I want food.' That was his immediate requirement. Food is so very important to mankind. We miss food only when we don't have it.

THE BEST IS YET TO BE

When you have something frugal, do not feel dejected as God will surely give you something great in life. Wait for sometime as God has a plan for everything and all of us. Hope for the best.

◆◆◆

13

DROP THINGS THAT DON'T WORK FOR YOU

Many of us sit and do things that don't work for us. We must try out more than one thing in order to pitch ourselves in one field. If we do well we can go on with it, but if we don't do well we have to think of some alternative than do the same thing. In this case we are to be blamed.

Man tries many things in life, especially when it comes to doing business or selecting his job. Well if a person is well placed in a Government job, he cannot switch over to some other job. A person doing a private job can afford to switch over to another job if he pleases. Same is the case with business. If a person does not do well in his business he has to do two things, one is he has to switch over to start a new one or he has to persevere and wait till his day comes. That is precisely what I have done in my business. I was doing very bad and now I have completely recovered and am doing very well in business.

Everything will not work for everybody. There are several reasons and some of them are, all of us can't do everything. To do different things we need to have a different set of mentalities and personalities. A very typical example is a person who wants to start a shop selling meat must be stone-hearted, he must not have sympathy for the birds and animals that he is slaughtering. Similarly a person running a restaurant must know about hygiene and also about preparation of foods and the taste that is required for people.

All of us must dream and have some vision to do something great. It could be either becoming something or achieving success in life. We can plan to take up a career as a scientist, an engineer or a doctor. On the other hand we may want to do our own business or invest in shares or get into some trading.

One must understand three important things in life.

They are:

1. To do a job - you need certain qualities
2. To do business - you need certain acumen
3. The third most important thing is - that we must do something.

To do a job, you need certain qualities: To do a job, all we need is a little bit of knowledge and commitment including ownership. I have mentioned in one of the chapters of this book that to be an employee we have to know certain things. Those things are, we have to love our profession, we have to be punctual and do what is given to us without being told. Such things are essential to do a job.

To do business also you need certain acumen: To do business we need a plan, we need finance and we need to have special qualities to do it. A person who is timid cannot do finance business; he has to be tough and shrewd to recover money. At the same time if a person is timid, he can still do some business that does not involve toughness. A person may start a departmental store or a medical shop.

The third most important thing is that we must do something: If we just sit, we will neither take a job nor give excuses that we are not selected and when it comes to business we do the wrong thing not suited for us and finally land up in loss. Hence we have to do something that matches our mentality.

I have known several people and also have friends and relatives who do nothing but just sit and either waste time doing nothing, or wait for someone to give them money. Many people sit and collect rent and interest from people and make a living. I feel it is important for people to do something in life rather than sit and waste time and do nothing.

When I say, 'Drop things that don't work for you.' I mean to say, we carry on with the same thing when we know we are not good at it. I would like to give you an example. A childhood friend of mine wanted to be a pilot. He began nurturing his dreams from a very small age by drawing aeroplanes, making models and even constructing a small aeroplane in jute cloth and bamboo and made a seat for himself and would play in it.

All along we were happy he was going to do some innovation or break a record in the aviation industry. But he began to digress from his main path and took to other things in between. He did get a couple of opportunities to go abroad, but turned it down as he felt that his career was made in the Indian Air force. In the meanwhile his mind was not focused and he began to drift away from his thoughts. He somehow managed to get going with his dream, but so many things happened in between. His father died and left behind no fortune. He had a younger brother and sister to look after. He was the only hope in his family.

He took up a job in an agency just to make a livelihood. He could not get along with those people as he was under tremendous pressure to work. He quit that place too and joined a cinema theatre as a ticket assistant. He could not withstand the pressure there too. He sought help from one of his uncles and tried a small business. He was living on a hand-to-mouth basis, till one day even that business crashed as there were larger players in the field.

What he thought would be his career was letting him down. He was nearly thirty years of age and was failing in health. He had lost total focus and then began thinking so many things; as a result his mind could not work properly. Many of us told him to give up his idea, but he still lives with it hoping that some day he would do well. He is hoping against hope that his dream will come true, but it is too late. That is why I say that if things don't work for you, it is time that you give it up and go for something new.

I shall give you my own example of how things did not work for me. I was employed in a company where we had a lot of crooks. I was too tough a person to handle and as result no one would listen to me. I was also not in the habit of unnecessarily bowing in front of my bosses. I was at the crossroads not knowing what to do. I had two choices; one was to be in the company of crooks and do what they did, which I was actually not in favour of. The other choice was to remain alone and just be a mute spectator. I did the latter.

This went on for some time till I realised I was also getting a bad name and hence I decided to quit and start my own company. The first attempt was a failure as I could not withstand market pressures and had no money to keep my business going. My associates whom I trusted most let me down very badly by joining my competitors. I decided to drop what was not good for me. I remained in hibernation for nearly two years. All along I kept writing books, novels and articles.

Now I run my own company which is moving towards greater heights and I feel my management is right. I have no issues with the people who work with me, if at all there are any hitches; they are small and negligible ones which does not count at all. I am heading my own company and doing very well in India.

STORY

Change your strategy when something does not go your way. One day, there was a blind man sitting on the steps of a building with a begging bowl by his feet and a sign that read:

'I am blind, please help.'

Lot of people passed by him but no one was interested in giving any money to him. The whole day he was sitting and he got only very few coins.

This was being watched by a creative artist working in an advertising agency. He felt pity for the poor blind man, went to him and put a few coins into the bowl and without asking for his permission, he took the sign, turned it around, and wrote another announcement. He placed the sign by his feet and left.

That afternoon the creative artist returned to the blind man and noticed that his bowl was full of coins. The blind man recognised his footsteps and asked if it was him who had re-written his sign and he wanted to know what he wrote on it?

The artist responded: 'Nothing that was not true, I just rewrote your sign differently.'

He smiled and went on his way. The blind man never knew but his new sign read: 'Today is Deepawali and I cannot see the lights.'

Change your strategy when something does not go your way and you'll see it will probably be for the best.

Have faith that every change is best for our lives. Only thing we need to remember is to look at things differently.

THOUGHT

Helen Prommel says:
'Turn stumbling blocks into stepping stones.
That make his going tough.
Can turn themselves to stepping stones,
If he steps high enough.
But if he thinks them stumbling blocks,
He'll surely hurt his bones;
While if he tries to walk on them,
He can make them stepping stones.
For he who learns from obstacles
To lengthen out his stride,
Can mount his stumbling blocks, and walk
Upon their upper side.'

THE BEST IS YET TO BE

When you fail in a particular area, do not worry as you will shine in some other area. There is nothing wrong in changing your line if it is not working for you, but remember sometimes in your failure lies your future success. Hope for the best.

◆◆◆

14

GOD IS THERE

There is enough proof to state that there is God. One may not have seen Him, but there is enough proof that He exists. There are disputes over His existence as people have made a mockery of making stone and other images just to make money. Hence many people do not believe in the existence of God.

You may be wondering as to why I have brought in God when I am writing a book 'The Best Is Yet To Be.' I believe in one thing and that is no man on this earth can do wonders and shine unless and until he has the blessings of God. It does not matter which God you believe in and whom you worship. There is a universal God who is in heaven and controls the earth and I believe in that God. I do not want to go into details of questions which others have to ask. This is one area that I avoid speaking to people about God. I believe in God and that is more than enough for me and I do not convince anybody and try to impress anybody about God. God is there, He is very much looking at us people and is in command of the universe and without His permission nothing will move.

Before I write this chapter, let me give you my view about God. I believe in God. I believe in the saints, I believe in the existence of angels and I also fully believe there is hell below us and heaven up above, where our ancestors and those who did noble deeds reside. I am also confident that I shall be with God, the saints, angels and my ancestors and friends one day.

Prayer is one form of interaction with God. Charles Dickens wrote the following letter to his youngest son who went out to Australia in 1868.

I need not tell you that I love you dearly and am very, very sorry in my heart to part with you. I have put a Holy Bible among your books because it is the best book that ever was, or will be, known in the world. As your brothers have gone away one by one I have written to each such word as I am now writing to you, entreating them all to guide themselves by this great book. Only one thing more, never abandon the practice of private prayer. I know the comfort of it.

Prayer will help to concentrate our thoughts if we pray in an orderly way. There are five different kinds of prayer:

They are:

1. The Prayer of approach
2. The Prayer of confession
3. The Prayer of thanksgiving
4. The Prayer of petition
5. The Prayer of intercession.

The Prayer of Approach: In the prayer of approach, we make ourselves aware of the presence of God around us and about us.

The Prayer of Confession: In the prayer of confession we ask God forgiveness for the wrong things that we have done.

The Prayer of Thanksgiving: In the prayer of thanksgiving we give thanks for the many blessings with which we are surrounded.

The Prayer of Petition: In the prayer of petition we bring our own special needs and desires to God.

The Prayer of Intercession: In the prayer of intercession we pray for other people.

Serenity Prayer:

God, Grant me the SERENITY to accept the things I cannot change,
The COURAGE to change the things I can,
and the WISDOM to know the difference.

In-a-lighter-vein

One person to the other - 'How come you're always running around looking for God? He's not lost.'

Many people around us do not believe in the existence of God.

Some people say, 'God is over-burdened with many things.'

While some other people say, 'God is busy in some areas.'

A lot of people say, 'That God does not exist.'

It all depends on how we take it. All said and done God is there; He exists and gives judgement to all. When you see some people suffering, that does not mean God is out to take revenge. He is only putting them to test. God takes man into deep waters to cleanse and never to drown him. That is the plain truth.

An atheist friend of mine mocks at God, yet when his wife goes to the temple, he says, 'Please pray for my success.'

Strange But True

In a small town, a person decided to open up a brothel, which was right opposite a Church. The Church and its congregation started a campaign to block the brothel from opening with petitions and prayed daily against this business.

Work progressed. However, when the brothel was almost complete and about to open, a strong lightning struck the brothel and it was burnt to the ground.

The Church folks were rather smug in their outlook after that, till the brothel owner sued the Church authorities on the grounds that the Church through its congregation and prayers was ultimately responsible for the destruction of his brothel, either through direct or indirect actions or means.

In its reply to the court, the Church vehemently denied all responsibility or any connection that their prayers were reasons for the act of God. As the case made its way into court, the judge looked over the paperwork at the hearing and commented:

'I don't know how I'm going to decide this case, but it appears from the paperwork, we have a brothel owner who believes in the power of prayer and we have an entire Church that doesn't.'

God Says

When you are sad
I will dry your tears.

When you are scared
I will comfort your fears.

When you are worried
I will give you hope.

When you are confused
I will help you cope.

And when you are lost and can't see the light,
I shall be your beacon shining ever so bright.

This is my oath
I pledge till the end.

Why you may ask?
Because I created you and I need to see you be happy.

Signed:
GOD

STORY

A man was sleeping at night in his cabin when suddenly his room was filled with light and God appeared. The Lord told the man He had work for him to do and showed him a large rock in front of his cabin.

The Lord explained that the man was to push against the rock with all his might. So, this the man did, day after day. For many years he toiled from sun up to sun down, his shoulders set squarely against the cold, massive surface of the unmoving rock, pushing with all of his might.

Each night the man returned to his cabin sore and worn out, feeling that his whole day had been spent in vain. Since the man was showing discouragement, the Adversary (Satan), decided to enter the picture by placing thoughts into the weary mind:

'You have been pushing against that rock for a long time, and it hasn't moved.' Thus, he gave the man the impression that the task was impossible and that he was a failure. These thoughts discouraged and disheartened the man.

Satan said, 'Why kill yourself over this? Just put in your time, giving just the minimum effort, and that will be good enough. That's what the weary man planned to do, but decided to make it a matter of prayer and to take his troubled thoughts to the Lord. 'Lord,' he said, 'I have laboured long and hard in your service, putting all my strength to do that which you have asked.

Yet, after all this time, I have not even budged that rock by half a millimetre. What is wrong? Why am I failing?' The Lord responded compassionately, 'My friend, when I asked you to serve Me and you accepted, I told you that your task was to push against the rock with all of your strength, which you have done.

Never once did I mention to you that I expected you to move it. Your task was to push. And now you come to me with your strength spent, thinking that you have failed. Is that really so? Look at yourself. Your arms are strong and muscled, your back sinewy and brown; your hands are callused from constant pressure, your legs have become massive and hard.

Through opposition you have grown much, and your abilities now surpass that which you used to have. True, you haven't moved the rock. But your calling was to be obedient and to push and to exercise your faith and trust in my wisdom. That you have done. Now I, my friend, will move the rock.'

At times, when we hear a word from God, we tend to use our own intellect to decipher what He wants, when actually what God wants is just a simple obedience and faith in Him. By all means, exercise the faith that moves mountains, but know that it is still God who moves mountains. When everything seems to go wrong...just P.U.S.H.! When the job gets you down... just P.U.S.H.! When people don't react the way you think they should... just P.U.S.H. When your money is 'gone' and the bills are due... just P.U.S.H!

When people just don't understand you... just P.U.S.H.

P= Pray
U= Until
S= Something
H= Happens

Let me end up this chapter with a beautiful story. An atheist Professor was teaching metaphysics. He was trying to drive home a point that God did not exist. Most of the students were upset, at the way in which he said God was not there. He went on with his lecture and suddenly found students who raised their hands. The Professor asked, 'What now?' The students asked the Professor, 'How can you prove that God is not there?' The Professor replied, 'If God is there He must come down and touch me on my cheek.' The student got up, went up to the Professor and gave him a hard slap and said, 'God wanted me to give you a rap on your face.' Now do you...?'

In-a-lighter-vein

One of the basic difference between God and human is; God gives- gives- gives. Human gets - gets - gets and finally forgets.

THE BEST IS YET TO BE

Many people curse God when they are in distress. People also ask questions 'we wonder if God is there'. Yes. God is very much there, He is present and watches over everyone. He loves us and He will always give us something, at times - late. Hope for the best.

◆◆◆

15

SIMPLY THE BEST

We have to appreciate whatever we have today, be it the world, the stars, the sky, the sea or the natural facilities that are given to us. We have to be happy with all that. Just imagine if we do not get water and the soil stops giving us grains or the trees giving us fruits. Hence we have to appreciate everything that we have as the best.

We live in a world full of scorpions and we do not know when we will get a sting. We have to carry the anti-sting medicine because we do not know when we will get it from someone who is not interested in our success or well-being. In such a world you will find many good people. I have known a mother who was deserted by her husband who was a dipsomaniac. She had a small infant whom she had to feed. She went round the country side and found nothing to eat, till she came to a pool where she spotted some fish. What do you think the woman did? She removed a part of her flesh and used it to catch fish to eat and gave milk for her child. Unbelievable but yet very true.

You have the ability to play the game of life. Think of the person who sits down to play the piano and all he can do is play discordant notes. As he plays, there is no harmony, no balance and no real tune, he hits all the wrong notes. The player eventually gets fed up with disharmony, lack of pleasure and lack of beauty and decides to go to a teacher. The teacher says, 'You have the ability to play, but you need to understand music.' 'Each one of us has the ability to play the game of life with balance, harmony and joy, but we need to know the rules and the principles', says Robert Anthony.

When we are at home, we grumble at the food, the place we sleep and also make a mountain out of a molehill where small things are concerned. That is because we have been brought up in such a manner. We undergo a mental conditioning at home and when we step out of our house we expect the same from others. Sometimes we get it and at times we do not get it.

Easy it is

Easy is to get a place in someone's address book.
Difficult is to get a place in someone's heart.

Easy is to judge the mistakes of others
Difficult is to recognise our own mistakes

Easy is to talk without thinking
Difficult is to refrain the tongue

Easy is to hurt someone who loves us.
Difficult is to heal the wound...

Easy is to ask for forgiveness
Difficult is to forgive others

Easy is to set rules.
Difficult is to follow them...

Easy is to dream every night.
Difficult is to fight for a dream...

Easy is to show victory.
Difficult is to assume defeat with dignity...

Easy is to admire a full moon.
Difficult to see the other side...

Easy is to stumble with a stone.
Difficult is to get up...

Easy is to enjoy life every day.
Difficult is to give its real value...

Easy is to promise something to someone.
Difficult is to fulfil that promise...

Easy is to say we love.
Difficult is to show it every day...

Easy is to criticise others.
Difficult is to improve oneself...

Easy is to make mistakes.
Difficult is to learn from them...

Easy is to weep for a lost love.
Difficult is to take care of it so as not to lose it.

Easy is to think about improving.
Difficult is to stop thinking it and put it into action...

Easy is to think bad of others
Difficult is to give them the benefit of the doubt...

Easy is to receive
Difficult is to give

Easy is to keep the friendship with words
Difficult is to keep it with meanings.

Easy to read this
Difficult to follow

One day I happened to visit an old friend of mine. He asked me specifically to meet him around noon. I went to see him and was surprised to see him offering me lunch which was prepared by his wife. The dishes were laid out and we began eating it.

His wife asked me, 'How is the food preparation?'

Even before I could answer, my friend interrupted and said, 'Please ask me that question and not the guest.'

His wife a little shocked asked him, 'Okay, how is the preparation?'

My friend began pointing out different mistakes in each dish. This statement of his made her very sad.

She turned to me and asked me a question, 'Is that true?'

I smiled and said, 'Everything is fine, except one thing.'

She was curious and asked, 'What is one thing?'

With a smile I said, 'Something must be wrong with your husband's taste-buds.'

Everyone including my friend's parents had a hearty laugh.

My friend also laughed and told me, 'Now I see the logic in your statement.'

After lunch we went to the terrace to have a smoke, we were discussing various things.

I told him, 'Never discourage anyone.'

I then asked my friend, 'Did you ever help her during her cooking in the kitchen which lasted about three hours?'

He smiled and said, 'I see your point is good, I shall appreciate and also help her in the kitchen when I find time.'

How Beautiful

There was a blind girl who hated herself because of her blindness. Not only did she hate herself but she hated everyone else, except her loving boyfriend. He was always there for her.

She said that if she could only see the world, she would marry her boyfriend.

One day, someone donated a pair of eyes to her and then she could see everything, including her boyfriend.

Her boyfriend asked her, 'Now that you can see the world, will you marry me?' The girl was shocked when she saw that her boyfriend was blind too, and refused to marry him.

Her boyfriend walked away in tears, and later wrote a letter to her that simply said. 'Just take care of my eyes dear.'

This is how a man changes when his status changes. Only a few remember what life was like before and even fewer remember who to thank for always being there even when times were painfully unbearable.

Parable

One day, a fisherman was walking along the sea-shore. He saw a young handsome man walking along the shore. The young man was picking the fish and throwing it into the water. The tiny fish had been washed by the waves to the shore.

The fisherman stood for a while to see what the man was up to. He then walked up to the young man and curiously asked, 'Young man, there are so many fishes lying here and so many are coming. What difference can you make to them; you are just a single person.'

The young man smiled at the fisherman and picked up one more fish and threw it into the sea and said, 'I made a difference to the life of this fish.'

For sometime the fisherman did not understand what the young man had said. But when he saw the man went on doing it. He then realised what the young man was up to and walked away.

I now reside in Coimbatore in Tamilnadu. I am used to drinking tea or coffee which is not too hot, I like to make it a little cold and drink. When I go to a tea-shop I request the 'tea-master' to make it a little cool.

Most of them do it, but at times some men say, 'We do not have the time as so many people are there.'

We have to put up with such things in our day to day life. When we go to a restaurant and order food, we do not get the food cooked the way we like, we just get what is cooked and served to us. We cannot grumble at what is served, we can do it at home. Hence we have to ensure that we are as flexible as possible.

STORY

Why do men lie? One day, while a woodcutter was cutting a branch of a tree above a river, his axe fell into the river. He began crying out loudly, so loudly that even God heard his cry. The Lord appeared to the woodcutter and asked, 'Why are you crying, my son?'

The woodcutter replied that his axe had fallen into the water and that he needed the axe to make his living. The Lord went down into the water and reappeared with a golden axe. 'Is this your axe?' the Lord asked. The woodcutter replied, 'No.'

The Lord again went down and came up with a silver axe. 'Is this your axe?' The Lord asked. Again, the woodcutter replied, 'No.' The Lord went down again and came up with an iron axe. 'Is this your axe?' the Lord asked.

The woodcutter replied, 'Yes.' The Lord was pleased with the man's honesty and gave him all three axes to keep, and the woodcutter went home happy. Some time later the woodcutter was walking with his wife along the riverbank, and his wife fell into the river.

When he cried out, the Lord again appeared and asked him, 'Why are you crying?' 'Oh Lord, my wife has fallen into the water!' The Lord went down into the water and came up with Trisha. 'Is this your wife?' the Lord asked.

'Yes,' cried the woodcutter. The Lord was furious. 'You lied! That is an untruth!' The woodcutter replied, 'Oh, forgive me, my Lord. It is a misunderstanding.

You see, if I had said 'no' to Trisha, You would have come up with Asin. Then if I also said 'no' to her, you would have come up with my wife.

Had I then said 'yes,' you would have given all three to me? Lord, I am a poor man, and am not able to take care of all three wives, so that's why I said yes to Trisha.'

The moral of this story is: Whenever a man lies, it is for a good and honourable reason, and for the benefit of others.

THE BEST IS YET TO BE

The best at times for some of us will not come that easily, it will come as slowly as a snail. The best will rest, it will take deviations and at times it will also forget to come unless you remind it. Hope for the best.

◆◆◆

16

LIFE IS A GIFT

Cute is when a person's personality shines through his looks. Like in the way they walk, every time you see them you just want to run up and hug them. A warm smile can get you friends and also favours. Hence make it a point to make the best of life.

Life itself is a mystery, but wait as you are reading this book you have been endowed with life by God. I have also been given life by God and that is how I am in a position to write a book that you are reading. Life itself is a gift which we have got from God after a series of processes that take place, especially planting by a couple, the meeting of the single winner sperm and then finding its mate the ovum and joining to begin the process of a foetus and so on and so forth. Then comes the next step of the mother allowing it to grow in the womb and giving the to-be born child nutrition and care. The mother also ensures that the child is not harmed in any way. And finally the big day comes when the baby is out into the world as a human entity. If we look at all this, a single person emerges winner and that is 'You.'

Life is a gift of God. What we give to life is our gift to God. We fight through from the womb and emerge as winners to come into this world. The very fact that we have been bestowed with life itself is something that we must rejoice. Unfortunately many people make a misery of their lives and also create problems for others. Today we have wars, famine, floods; one person has got food in excess while the other is hard up even for one square meal. That is the irony of life. Yet, if we mind, we can make life a wonderful experience not only for us but for the others too.

'Lift up your thoughts and thereby lift your life.' A man will find that as he alters his thoughts towards things and other people, things and other people will alter towards him. Let a man radically alter his thoughts, and he will be astonished at the rapid transformation it will effect in the material conditions of his life. A man can only remain weak, abject and miserable by refusing to lift up his thoughts. One does not lose anything by lifting his thoughts, neither does he have to toil to do so. A person can dream and assume that he is even the President of India. Who can stop him in his mind from thinking big unless he himself plans to do so?

I must address this chapter to the people who say, 'Life is a bore and a burden.' We do not know if there is something called rebirth or if we take birth again. What we have heard from people is that we have nine or seven lives, but that is not proved. But one proof is there and that is we live here and now and hence we have to make it a point to live that life fully and not end it just because we have some difficulties.

As I am writing this book, a man in New Delhi committed suicide as rowdies of private bank had gone to his house and harassed him and his family members. I do not understand why this man had to end his life. He could have very well lived his life and either paid up the money he owed to this bank or could have also mustered strength and support met people and could have made a group to thrash those rowdies who were out to take his life. If I had an opporunity to meet this man I would have surely motivated him to live. I too had the same problem with a bank some years ago. Today I am in such a position that persons from the same bank keep calling me offering credit cards and requesting me to invest in their bank. I however ignore their calls.

My message here is that one must not end life but instead face realities and stand firm and wait for that day to shine in life. Just imagine how many sperms and ovum's would have had the dream of becoming a human being, they were all destroyed in the process of the formation of you and me.

Life has many faces. For someone life is full of pain and for many others life is full of enjoyment. Actually, 'your life is what you want it to be.' Life can be planned. I hope you will make life a celebration rather than pain and agony.

Life should be an exciting adventure for you. The sun should rise within you each day in terms of the richness of your feelings and the sharpness of your perceptions. You should carve out goals for yourself that will inspire you to enthusiastic action. Going towards life with vigour, no matter what your age, you should never fear death.

Improve the quality of life. As efficiency means a higher percentage of result. By result we mean a large number of things – wealth, health, achievement, fame, friendship, happiness, knowledge, character. There are at least a hundred points on which we might give a man marks for efficiency, in estimating the quality of his life.

Quote

That is the beauty of life filled with wonderful golden moments. There are moments in life when you miss someone so much that you just want to pick them from your dreams and hug them for real!

When the door of happiness closes, another opens; but often times we look so long at the closed door that we don't see the one which has been opened for us.

Think Again

Today before you think of saying an unkind word
Think of someone who can't speak.

Before you complain about the taste of your food
Think of someone who has nothing to eat.

Before you complain about your spouse
Think of someone who's crying out to God for a companion.

Today before you complain about life
Think of someone who died too early.

Before you complain about your children
Think of someone who desires children but they're barren.

Before you argue about your dirty house
Think of the people who are living in the streets.

Before whining about the distance you drive
Think of someone who walks the same distance with their feet.

And when you are tired and complain about your job
Think of the unemployed, the disabled and those who wished they had your job.

But before you think of pointing the finger or condemning another
Remember that not one of us is without sin and we all answer to God.

And when depressing thoughts seem to get you down
Put a smile on your face and thank God you're alive and still around.

Life is a gift, live it, enjoy it, celebrate it, and fulfil it.

Tit Bit

To realise the value of ONE YEAR
Ask a student who has failed his final exam.

To realise the value of ONE MONTH
Ask a mother who has given birth to a premature baby.

To realise the value of ONE WEEK
Ask an editor of a weekly newspaper.

To realise the value of ONE DAY
Ask a daily wage labourer who has ten kids to feed.

To realise the value of ONE HOUR
Ask the lovers who are waiting to meet or.

To realise the value of ONE MINUTE
Ask a person who has missed the train.

To realise the value of ONE SECOND
Ask a person who has survived an accident.

To realise the value of ONE MILLISECOND
Ask the person who has won a silver medal in the Olympics.

Treasure every moment that you have and treasure it more because you
Share it with someone special, special enough to have your time.
'It is our attitude and not aptitude that determines our altitude in life.'

In summing up – life gives you what you ask. I bargained with life for a penny, and life would pay no more. However I begged at evening, when I counted my scanty store. For life is just an employer, it gives you what you ask, but once you have set the wages you must bear the task. I worked for a meagre wage only to be dismayed. That any wage I asked of life, life would have willingly paid.

What life should mean to you?
According to William A Ward
Life is not as much...
A fight to be fought
A game to be played
A race to be run
A prize to be shared

Life is more dearly.
God's will to be sought
A course to be laid
A work to be done
A gift to be shared.

Life I must say is the best gift that we get from God, it becomes our duty to live it righteous and fulfil what the creator wants us to do and also leave our footprints on the sands of time. We must never forget that we have to make our stay on this earth a pleasant one and not a pain for anyone. After all who knows if we will ever get another opportunity to live life again.

THE BEST IS YET TO BE

When I say life is a gift, let us not assume that life will always be a bed of roses. It will also be a bush of thorns for us at times. If you want life to be a gift, lead life righteously, be creative, get yourself well-equipped and do what God wills. Hope for the best.

◆◆◆

17

ALL FOR THE BEST

Whatever happens in life is for our own good. If we have a failure that is a warning. If there is a setback that is a sign that it is a rider to get ready. If we have poverty, that is a lesson for us. If we have a jolt it means we have to be steady; if we get a piece of bad news that means we have to prepare for the worst. Hence whatever happens is for our own good.

Life is a gift of God and there are many things that happen in life. For some life is good, for many life is bad and for several people life is something difficult to live. People live in pain and misery. Life is also a series of choices. On one side you can choose certain things – a car, a spouse, a book, etc. But on the other side you cannot choose certain things – your parentage, fate, race and colour.

One logic we have to follow is to make the best choice when things are in our hands. Before that, let us get to know what is in our hands and what is in the hands of God.

What is in the hands of God?

1. Your birth
2. Your gender
3. Your looks
4. The fate

5. The body constitution
6. Longevity
7. Karmas.

Your Birth: You may be born in a slum or you may be born in a palace. You may take your birth in a prosperous country like India or America or you may even be born in a war torn and poor country like Somalia or Ethiopia. You cannot choose it.

Your Gender: When we are in our mother's womb, our gender is determined. We cannot make a change or bargain for a change in gender, we have to come out of the womb as we are created inside. There is no concession here. Today we have people changing their genders, that is artificial and not natural.

Your Looks: You may be dark; you may be fair; you may be thin or fat. That again depends on how you are created. Some are handsome and beautiful; some are ugly and have bad looks. That is the way we have been created.

The Fate: This is something that confuses me, I leave that decision to my readers as to whether he/she believes in fate or he/she believes that we can steer our lives. But still there is evidence of the fact that there is fate or are there factors beyond our control. We call it a mystery.

The Body Constitution: Some of us are tall; many short, some are blind, many are lame. All this is not decided by us but our Creator.

Longevity: This is something that I differ on but yet, let me state that it largely depends on how we look at it. We can either prolong our lives by being positive, even if we are in a negative situation or we can cut it short by smoking, excessive drinking and burdening our hearts. But at the same time we must not stop from living a healthy life just because someone tells us that we will die young.

Karmas: This is a theory which has not been proved. We only believe what the scriptures and elders say. Most of the people who speak about *Karma* are the ones who have either half-baked knowledge or assume things. To some extent it may be true. But that should not stop a person from achieving something outstanding in his life.

What is in our hands?

1. Our Well-being
2. Career
3. Life
4. Choice to be glad or sad
5. Choice to make a living the way we want
6. Choice to be an asset or a burden
7. Choice to live an ordinary life or leave footprints.

Our Well-being: We can decide on our well-being. We can either be liked or disliked. We can decide to conduct ourselves well and get a good name or we can choose to behave badly and make people detest us.

Career: We can choose any career we want. We can take up a Government job and languish for the rest of our lives and yet live securely or we can do our own business by taking a risk and either flourish or perish.

Life: Our life is in our own hands; we can make it or break it. We can make a success story of our life or we can even make a misery of our life. That entirely depends on us.

Choice to be glad or sad: Every day we wake up and have two choices to make. One choice is to be 'happy.' The alternative choice is to be 'sad.' We can make a choice to be happy and enjoy. We can also choose to be sad and have a gloomy day. That decision entirely depends on us.

Choice to make a living the way we want: We can live in penury or we can even live in opulence. We can spend lavishly and beg at the end of the day or we can save and be secure. That choice is ours.

A popular prologue says, 'If you are born poor it's not your fault, but if you die poor then that is your foolishness.'

Choice to be an asset or a burden: Many people do nothing and are a burden to their parents, relatives or siblings. At the same time they can decide to contribute to society in any small manner that they can.

Did not an old couple plant saplings for the new generation to reap the fruits? Story in chapter 4.

Choice to live an ordinary life or leave our footprints in the sands of eternity: Many people were born during the time of Swami Vivekananda, but why we don't remember them? That is because they lived an ordinary life, whereas Swamiji was determined to leave his footprints on the sands of time before he departed.

Ultimately I wish to say that whatever happens is for our own good. We have to take things the way it comes to us.

> 'I was in blues for I had no shoes, till I saw a person without feet.' We grumble for small things, some of us do it at the drop of a hat.

Cute Comparisons

We go to a restaurant and find fault with the food, while someone does not have anything to eat.

We complain about water while some people don't have even a drop to drink.

We complain about the noise which disturbs us, yet there are people living on the noisy roads all day long.

We complain about so many things without looking at what life is on the other side.

If one is sensible, he will pause for a while and have logic in his mind before he grumbles.

Never grumble,
whatever happens,
whatever has happened,
and whatever is going to happen
is all for our own good.

You'll be Stunned

A jobless man applied for the position of 'office boy' at a huge software company. The Human Resources Manager interviewed him and then watched him cleaning the fioor as a test.

'You are employed.' He said. 'Give me your email address and I'll send you the application to fill in, as well as date when you may start.'

The man replied 'But I don't have a computer, neither an email.'

'I'm sorry', said the Human Resources Manager, 'If you don't have an email, you do not exist. And one who doesn't exist, cannot have the job.'

The man left with no hope at all. He didn't know what to do, with only rupees 10 in his pocket. He then decided to go to the super market and bought a kilogram of tomatoes. He then sold the tomatoes in a door to door round.

In less than two hours, he succeeded to double his capital. He repeated the operation three times, and returned home with rupees 60. The man realised that he could survive by this way, and started to go everyday earlier, and return late. Thus his money doubled or tripled every day. Shortly, he bought a cart, then a truck, and then he had his own fleet of delivery vehicles.

About five years later, the man became one of the biggest food retailers in the town. He started to plan his family's future, and decided to have a life insurance. He called an insurance broker, and chose a protection plan. When the conversation was concluded, the broker asked him his email. The man replied, 'I don't have an email'.

The broker answered curiously, 'You don't have an email, and yet have succeeded to build an empire. Can you imagine what you could have been if you had an email?'

The man thought for a while and replied, 'Yes, I'd be an office boy at a Software Company.'

Moral of the story: Whatever happens is for the best. Take things as they come without getting dejected in life.

THOUGHT

Living on earth is expensive, but it does include a free trip around the sun every year.

How long a minute is, depends on what side of the bathroom door you're on.

Birthdays are good for you; the more you have, the longer you live.

Happiness comes through doors you didn't even know you left open.

Ever notice that the people who are late are often much jollier than the people who have to wait for them?

Most of us go to our grave with our music still inside us.

A righteous man is like the sandalwood tree which gives fragrance even to the axe that cuts it.

You may be only one person in the world, but you may also be the world to one person.

Some mistakes are too much fun to make only once.

Don't cry because it's over; smile because it has happened.

We could learn a lot from crayons: some are sharp, some are pretty, some are dull, some have weird names, and all are different colours....but they all exist very nicely in the same box.

A truly happy person is one who can enjoy the scenery on a detour.

Have an awesome day, and know that someone who thinks you're wonderful, has thought about you today! 'And that person is me.'

THE BEST IS YET TO BE

Whatever happens in life is for our own good. We may meet with failures, we may come across hurdles. We may lose a loved one. We may have losses in business, but remember whatever happens is for the best. Hope for the best.

◆◆◆

18

THE SUFFERING PHASE

At one time or the other we all suffer in life. Suffering is such a misery that no one wants to undergo. I am speaking about the long suffering that man undergoes. This generally happens for a period of seven to ten years in one's life time. I have also come across people who have suffered all their lives and gone to the grave with a heavy heart.

It is believed and it is also true that the darkest part of the night leads to dawn. This is not only true but it has happened and is happening to many people in their lives. I have tried to introspect as to why such bad times come to us. I have not found an answer to this question. Several people have given their views about it but I am not convinced as they all have their own opinions.

Benjamin Franklin said:

'There will be plenty of time to sleep when you are dead. Hence life is meant for living. So wake up perform your duties when you are yet alive for after you die you cannot do anything as your brain and body will be dead and will gradually disintegrate. This is a chance for man to do what he is poised to do when he is alive and not when he is dead and gone as the maggots will do what you don't want when you are in your death-sleep.'

All those who gave me their reasons made me believe what they told was true, but I had my own reservations. I have not found an answer to this problem. Here are the reasons quoted by people.

They are:

1. Lessons from God
2. Karma
3. Past Sins
4. Fate
5. Sins of Ancestors
6. Miscalculation
7. Suffering.

Lessons from God: Many people felt that it was done deliberately by God to teach man his lessons. God can teach man his lessons only by punishing him and giving him some anxious moments. Suffering is like gold that undergoes a great amount of heat before it is purified.

Karma: No one is sure of the law of *Karma*, it seems to exist but it has not been proved scientifically that it is true. However there is some substance in certain issues to believe that *Karma* exists and that is true. But it is advisable that people just hear it and not take things to their heart to live by it.

Past Sins: Many people feel that one suffers due to their own sins, that of their parents or ancestors. Those who sinned in the past may have done it unintentionally. Does that mean that his descendants should suffer? What mistake did they do to suffer? This is again a mystery.

Fate: Several people believe that it is fate that plays a role in one's suffering in life. Whatever has to happen will happen and no one can escape or change what is to occur. This is the perception of one group of people, it is better we take life positively rather than believe too much on fate.

Sins of Ancestors: It is a strong belief that we suffer due to the sins committed by our ancestors. This is just a belief and no concrete proof exists to prove that it is true.

Miscalculation: Our suffering can also be due to our miscalculation. All what we do and all what we think will not happen accordingly. So when we suffer it is due to our own miscalculation or our violation of natural laws.

Suffering: Suffering in life is a natural phenomena. But very few people rarely suffer. Why are they spared? Is it because they are lucky or that they are free from sin and that their ancestors have not sinned? This is also a mystery.

In-a-lighter-vein

A student was asked by a teacher, 'How many rings do men get when they get married?' The boy said, 'Well, the engagement-ring, the wedding-ring and of course suffer-ring.'

All suffering will come to an abrupt end when the suffering goes deeper and deeper. I had witnessed such an experience in my life time. Here's what happened to me during this time.They are:

1. I felt my world was closing in
2. All hope was lost
3. I lost appetite
4. I lost sleep
5. I felt my dreams shattered
6. I was contemplating suicide
7. I lost hope in life itself.

I felt my world was closing in: When I saw I was being cornered from all angles, I thought that I was the only one being cornered and that it was the dead end for me. All three miseries knocked my door, financiers, ill-health and poverty.

All hope was lost: Whatever little hope I had was all lost. My health was deteriorating, my mind would not function and I took to heavy smoking and drinking. A close friend of mine even said, 'I was going to become mad.'

I lost appetite: As such I had very little money to buy food and when I did have the money to buy some, I could not eat thinking of all these problems.

I lost sleep: Thinking of my problems, I lost sleep. My loss of appetite added injury to insult and I was wide awake and whenever I was awake I smoked cigarettes, which was my only solace.

I felt my dreams shattered: Since whatever I did, flopped. I thought that I was not capable of achieving anything in life and hence all my dreams were shattered. I started to get one bad news after the other.

I was contemplating suicide: One night I thought that I had already approached the end of the road and in order to avoid any more embarrassment I thought that the best way was to end my life and put an end to all my miseries.

Three things stopped me, one was the pain of committing suicide, second was my parents dream about me (they had fed, clothed and looked after me for twenty-three years). Lastly I thought, 'What if good days are going to come?'

I lost hope in life itself: Since life had treated me very badly, I thought that I must not respect life as it has given me all the worst things one can ever think of. Hence I thought that there was no hope in life. I felt life was offering to someone what was meant for me.

After all this I did not want to end my life. I was waiting for the angel of death to arrive and take me away. The angel did come, but it was not the angel of death, but the angel-of-hope, from that day till today, there is no looking back. Touchwood!

I used to wake up everyday with such an uncertainty, that I would wonder why at all there was another day. Today it is just the opposite. When I was suffering, an hour was very long for me, but today I feel an hour is too short. The time remains the same but my success has shortened the time. That makes all the difference.

I used to weep a lot and sit the whole day brooding over things. During this time not a single soul would either visit or even bother to help me. I was all alone. All I had was a small kitten that gave me company. I had very little food to eat but I ensured that the kitten was given something to eat. It used to sleep with me all night and would never go out anywhere. It was fond of me and waited till my arrival when I went out.

During my sufferings I tried a lot of things. I kept wondering what could be the reason for my fall from grace and the untold suffering.

I used to question myself, 'Did I anger God in any way that he is punishing me so badly?'

I had no answer. All my prayers went into deaf ears. Nothing worked. I tried several things.

They are:

1. Prayer Power
2. Change of God
3. Astrology
4. Using gems, stones and doing pujas
5. Changing the position of things at home.
6. Stopped worshipping God
7. Changed my business line.

Prayer Power: I tried very hard praying to God. Nothing worked. On one side I thought God was elsewhere listening to bigger problems. Secondly I thought that God was too busy as there were more people to whom he had to give attention.

Change of God: I strongly felt my God was busy and that I had to try smaller or lesser known gods. I even tried this and nothing worked out. Again I lost hope in God as I was desperate and wanted an instant reply. When I did not get it I thought that there was no God.

Astrology: I sought counsel from an astrologer who was a cheat. He told seventy five per cent good things about me and the rest twenty five per cent was negative about me. All he wanted was a big sum to do a pooja which I did not believe. I did lose some money but I learnt my lesson.

Using gems, stones and doing pujas: I tried using a gemstone, but nothing happened. I also tried doing a pooja to please the gods to draw their attention towards me, but nothing worked. My condition remained the same except for one thing, the little money I had was gone.

Changing the position of things at home: A close friend of mine brought a Vaasthu consultant who wanted me to pat him money even before he told anything. He suggested that I change the position of the cot, sofas and also the cooking area to bring luck. But even after a month nothing happened, things remained the same.

Stopped worshipping God: I was so vexed with God. Just above my house was a man who was thriving. He never went to any Temple, Mosque or a Church. He had no gemstones nor did he do any pooja, yet he was very successful. I stopped worshipping God and when I was in trouble I had to go to him.

Changed my business line: I sought help from my friend who said that my current business (training) was not suited for me and hence I changed my business. Things went even worse and hence I had to revert to training.

In spite of doing all these things nothing good happened. In the bargain I had borrowed money on interest and that too was getting over. I was now desperately losing hope. I saw things were taking a bad shape and getting worse.

Finally I came to a conclusion that bad times are inevitable and will not spare anyone whatsoever the reason may be. But if your time is bad, all you have to do is just sit there without moving. Nothing will happen, whatever you do, will remain the same. You will surely see good times. On the other hand if your time is good, no one can stop you from climbing up. You don't have to do anything. People will come in search of you, money will chase you and friends will queue up to see you. All the good will happen to you.

I just have one word to share with you, my readers, unlike others who are in their dark days. I did something which you will surely appreciate. That is I never gave up hope. All along I had some hope flickering in my mind. In this context what I did was to sit and write books. Many people made fun of me. They even termed me mad. But that madness had made me very famous and wanted person in society. Hence never waste your time when you are down and out. It will come handy one day when you are on top of the world.

THOUGHT

Remember what Napoleon Hill said, 'Success is dormant in every defeat. You are fortunate if you have learned the difference between temporary defeat and failure. More fortunate still if you have learned the truth that the very seed of success is dormant in every defeat that you experience.'

STORY

This story indicates that one must not relish sufferings. There was once a teacher of esotericism, who would surprisingly teach by just writing on the black-board instead of giving lectures to his students. One day he entered the classroom and wrote the following five sentences on the black-board for his students:
Stop loving your suffering,
Stop enjoying your persecution,

Stop adoring your anxiety,
Stop cherishing your resentment,
Stop glorifying your failure.

If you want spiritual rebirth, give up your love for such foolishness.

The teacher simply meant that you may think people want to end their suffering and persecution, but the fact remains that they fight like tigers to keep them.

The implication of this story is that people enjoy their suffering because suffering provides an excuse for egotism. The sufferer is able to remain in the centre of both his own attention and the attention of others.

THE BEST IS YET TO BE

No man is beyond suffering. Every human being however rich or powerful he may be, must and should suffer at some point or the other. The only ones who don't suffer are the people in the mental asylum or those who have taken refuge in God. Hope for the best.

◆◆◆

19

MUSINGS FROM A MILLIONAIRE

A millionaire is not a man with two brains or a twin-heart. He has the same brain as you and me and has got the same type and size of brain like any other person on this earth. What makes him special? Very simple, he is a person who is fond of money, he works for it, multiplies and has got his head over his shoulders when it comes to spending or investing his money.

No ordinary man can become a millionaire. If things are to be believed, one must be selected to be one and for that matter it is not an easy task to be one. It is also believed that one becomes a millionaire after what he had done in his previous birth and as such the virtue of being a millionaire is not bestowed upon everybody but only a select few. Unfortunately most millionaires are people who are basically misers who do not want to part with the money they have earned. Many millionaires, at least most of them have never earned the money through hard ways, they come up the wrong way by denying basic rights to the ones who work for them.

I was obsessed with millionaires and would long to see one. I would also read a lot of things about what makes a millionaire.

The only difference I saw in millionaires is their way of thinking. Millionaires are also of two types: Those who have inherited wealth from their ancestors and the others who have earned it on their own. Today we have a different category millionaires who have become rich overnight - they are our very own politicians.

What makes an ordinary person different from a millionaire? Millionaires are people with the same potential as you and me, the only difference is that they work differently. They plan their finances in such a way that they do not lose it.

Here's how a millionaire is different from the others. Their Qualities are:

1. Positive Thinkers
2. Wealth Conscious
3. Risk Takers
4. Invest in right things
5. They are very shrewd
6. They do planning
7. They believe in smart work alone

Positive Thinkers: The most successful people are the positive thinkers. They feel they can walk to the moon and the also make anything possible.

Wealth Conscious: Unless and until one is wealth-conscious, he will not have wealth at his disposal. Wealth comes only to those who beckon it.

Risk Takers: Achievers in life are surely the risk-takers. We have to take a risk to do something great in life.

Invest in right things: Many people invest, but very few invest in right things. Hence we have to invest in the right thing, at the right time and in the right place.

They are very shrewd: Most people who have money are very shrewd. I have a wealthy friend in Bangalore who will not hesitate to spend a couple of rupees for you and ask for it. In the beginning I felt he was shameless, but then I came to realise why he was in that position now.

They do planning: People who have succeeded have also been great planners. There are very few people who have not planned and have succeeded in life. These people plan their finances very well.

They believe in smart work alone: There are millions of people who do hard work. They hardly save any money. But there are also the smart people who work sharp and earn millions of rupees in a short span of time. Millionaires do hard and smart work.

Some of the millionaires who I have heard about and read are:

1. Bill Gates of Microsoft
2. Ray Croc of McDonalds
3. Hilton of Hilton Hotels
4. Walt Disney of Walt Disney Productions
5. Richard Branson of Virgin Group
6. Ross Perot, a Texas Oil Baron
7. Ted Turner of CNN.

Bill Gates: A very successful and shrewd businessman who founded Microsoft.

Ray Croc: The man who founded the McDonalds chain of restaurants all over the world.

Hilton: This is a man who set up the Hilton chain of hotels all over the world, a trend-setter in the Hospitality Industry.

Walt Disney: The man who brought great cartoon characters like Micky Mouse and Donald Duck, he went through fire to set up his empire called the Walt Disney Productions.

Richard Branson: The man who started several businesses and is quite successful, he is the founder of the Virgin Group.

Ross Perot: This man contested the American Presidential elections and lost, he is a great businessman and an Oil Baron from Texas.

Ted Turner: The man behind CNN, which is a premier global news channel in the world today.

These are only some of the names that I have mentioned. There are many more whose names I have not written. Most of them have come up the hard way. I do not wish to write the names of persons who have inherited wealth. They have not sown any seed; they are just nurturing the tree planted by their ancestors.

A millionaire also needs to decide whether to sow a seed to get a plant or a tree. If he plants a seed to just get a plant, he will get a yield and may have to sow again. There are also other millionaires who sow a seed and wait for it to grow into a huge tree. They enjoy the fruits for the rest of their lives. All they have to do is guard the tree against poachers.

Some call millionaires dirty people. They shower praises in front of them but they curse them behind their backs. Millionaires are people with a mentality 'who can break a stone with a glass,' type of attitude.

Today I am not obsessed with millionaires as I do not see anything great in them as I myself am on the way to becoming a millionaire. I have read the traits of millionaires and have mixed it up and put everything into practice. What I would like to say while I sum up is 'that a person who wants to become a millionaire needs certain USP's (Unique Selling Preposition)' according to me. They are:

1. Love for Money
2. Vision
3. Smart Work
4. A Costly and Gigantic Project
5. Difference in Thinking
6. Workaholic
7. Forward Thinking.

Love for Money: Unless a person has got love for money, he will not be in a position to amass wealth. He must be fond of money and must dream about money. He must be totally involved in earning money.

Vision: He must have a dream not only for himself but for his business or organisation. He must work towards a specific goal and must possess a vision and ensure that the others who work with him also follow it.

Smart Work: He must be a believer in smart work alone. No man who has worked hard has ever achieved anything in life. A person who works as a coolie does not have a big bank balance nor does a mason have a car as all these people use their body and not their brains to earn money.

A Costly and Gigantic Project: A person who owns a petty shop or a bakery cannot aim to be a millionaire. He must have a project that is running into several lakhs of rupees, only then can he think of earning in crores.

Difference in Thinking: A person who wants to be a millionaire must be a person who thinks differently. He must not be petty-minded and look for small money. He must have the patience to wait till his empire grows or he must do the right type of investment.

Workaholic: Unless a person is a workaholic, he cannot achieve his goal. He need not be a workaholic for the rest of his life. All he has to do is to lay the foundation and create a system which will take care of the super-structure.

Forward Thinking: A person who is forward in thinking will move ahead in life. If he is small-minded and looks at things narrowly, he cannot achieve great things in life.

A person who wants to amass wealth must be a 'master' and not a 'slave' because if he is a slave, he will have a restricted income and hence he cannot achieve his goals. If a person is a master he can run his own business as and how he likes. He can do what he feels like, unlike working for someone.

Testimony

There was a one hour interview on CNBC with Warren Buffet, the second richest man who has donated $31 billion (85% of his fortune) to charity.

Here are some very interesting aspects of his life:

He bought his first share at age 11 and he now regrets that he started too late!

He bought a small farm at age 14 with savings from delivering newspapers.

He still lives in the same small 3 bedroom house in mid-town Omaha, that he bought after he got married 50 years ago. He says that he has everything he needs in that house. His house does not have a wall or a fence.

He drives his own car everywhere and does not have a driver or security people around him.

He never travels by private jet although he owns the world's largest private jet company.

His company, Berkshire Hathaway, owns 63 companies. He writes only one letter each year to the CEOs of these companies, giving them goals for the year. He never holds meetings or calls them on a regular basis.

He has given his CEOs only two rules.

Rule number 1: Do not lose any of your share holder's money.

Rule number 2: Do not forget rule number 1.

He does not socialise with the elite of the society. His pastime after he gets home is to make himself some pop-corn and watch television.

Bill Gates, the world's richest man met him for the first time only 5 years ago. Bill Gates did not think he had anything in common with Warren Buffet. So he had scheduled his meeting only for half an hour. But when Gates met him, the meeting lasted for ten hours and Bill Gates became a devotee of Warren Buffet.

Warren Buffet does not carry a cell phone, nor has a computer on his desk.

His advice to young people: Stay away from credit cards and invest in yourself. Be modest!

In-a-lighter-vein

Generally people who amass wealth and have huge money are believed to be misers, but the saying goes like this. 'Misers are miserable people to live with, but they make great ancestors.'

THE BEST IS YET TO BE

To be a millionaire, it is not necessary that you are born with a star or a silver spoon in your mouth. A majority of the millionaires are made and not born. Programme your mind to be one and soon you will be a millionaire. Hope for the best.

◆◆◆

20

HOW TO STAY YOUNG

There are two things involved as far as the age is concerned. We grow in age and in spirit. One can be very old in age but young in spirit; he can be several years younger. That again depends on his attitude. A seventy year old man was seen wearing a T-shirt and said, 'I am fifty years of age with twenty years of experience.' That is what we call attitude.

There is great joy if a person stays young, one of the aspects is he/she can do what he/she wants in life. One cannot expect an old person to enjoy life like the way the young do and hence many people prefer to remain or for that matter like to look young. That is why you see people dying their hair and moustache to look young.

How to look young? It is based on three factors.

They are:

1. Our habits
2. The food we eat
3. The way we conduct ourselves in life.

Our habits: The way in which we utilise time, the time we wake up and also the time we sleep apart from our habits like smoking, drinking and other addictions will constitute how old we become in life.

The food we eat: The food we eat matters a lot. If we eat the right foods at the right time and with the right proportion and quantity that will also have a say in our age, looks and structure.

The way we conduct ourselves in life: Many of us live with problems. Some of us are in the habit of doing and speaking unnecessary things that harm not only us but also the person(s) we are speaking about. This bad habit also can tell much about how we look.

And of course the last point is how we look at things. Laughing, having fun, taking things very lightly, helping people and keeping the body fit and mind firm can play a role in how we look.

Once when I was travelling from Chennai to Bangalore in a Volvo bus, I had the privilege of interacting with a woman who was seated next to me. As we picked up a conversation, we got to know each other. I asked her what she was doing. She looked like she was in her thirties. She shocked me saying that she had a grand daughter and when I enquired about her age she said she was fifty five.

I could not believe what she said, but then again she said, 'I have only come across women who reduce their age and have rarely come across persons who reveal their actual age.'

I then came to a conclusion that she would have led a good life and that was why she looked young.

The young man who looked old

I observe two things in the world today. Once when I saw a handsome young man who looked very old, I wondered why he looked so. This man had a plethora of problems to tell me. I had to literally run away when he said it would take three days to complete his sad story.

When I first spoke to the man who was about forty years of age, he looked like he was sixty years and had hardly any stamina left. His face looked sullen, he had grey hair and his eyes were deep into his skull. One could make out that he was old, weak and was feeling miserable in his looks.

He said, 'When man is about forty he begins to get all the ailments, which I have. The world is bad and there is a lot of pollution. The food is bad and the water is contaminated. Wherever I go I see bad people and things also are pretty bad.'

I felt that he was looking old because this was the way he looked at the world.

This is the reason why he looked old. He looked at life negatively.

The old man who looked young

On the other side I saw an old man who was more than sixty years of age, he looked as if he was forty. When I spoke to him, he smiled at me and appreciated whatever was around him. He liked the sunshine; he appreciated nature. He enjoyed his food and thanked God for every little thing.

He smiled and said, 'It is not necessary that we condition our mind that we are old. When old age comes, we have to fight it and must not give in, when we give in, old age sets in. I am quite content in my life. I eat the right food; I wake up early and sleep late. I don't find fault with nature, I have learnt to fight odds of life. The one thing I learnt in life is never to brood over anything. When milk is spilt or spoilt, I try to bring fresh milk rather that fretting and fuming. I pray, meditate and live on hopes. That is keeping me going even at this age.'

This positive thinking is the reason why he was looking so young.

Stay Young

1. *Throw out non-essential numbers. This includes age, weight, and height. Let the doctors worry about them. That is why you pay them.*
2. *Keep only cheerful friends. Avoid bad-tempered people. They tend to pull you down.*
3. *Keep learning more about the computers, crafts, gardening, etc. Never let the brain get idle. 'An idle mind is the devil's workshop.'*
4. *Enjoy the simple things.*
5. *Laugh often, long and loud. Laugh until you gasp for breath. And if you have a friend who makes you laugh, spend lots and lots of time with him or her.*
6. *At times tears are required, grieve, and move on. The only person who is with you throughout your entire life, is you. Live while you are alive.*
7. *Surround yourself with what you love, whether it's family, pets, music, plants, hobbies, etc. Your home is your refuge.*
8. *Keep a tab on your health, preserve it. If it is unstable, improve it. If it is beyond what you can improve, get help.*
9. *Don't take guilt trips. Take a trip to the mall, even to a foreign country, but not to where you feel guilty.*
10. *Tell people you love that you love them, at every opportunity.*

STORY

One day a farmer's donkey fell into a well. The animal cried piteously for hours, as the farmer tried to figure out what to do. Finally, he decided the animal was old and the well needed to be covered up anyway. It just wasn't worth it to retrieve the donkey.

He invited all his neighbours to come over and help him. They all grabbed a shovel and began to shovel dirt into the well.

At first, the donkey realised what was happening and cried horribly. Then, to everyone's amazement he became quiet.

A few shovel loads later, the farmer finally looked down the well and was astonished at what he saw.

With every shovel of dirt that hit his back, the donkey was doing something amazing. He would shake it off and take a step up. As the farmer's neighbours continued to shovel dirt on top of the animal, he would shake it off and take a step up. Pretty soon, everyone was amazed, as the donkey stepped up over the edge of the well and trotted off.

Life is going to shovel dirt on you, all kinds of dirt. The trick to getting out of the well is to shake it off and take a step up. Each of our troubles is a stepping stone. We can get out of the deepest wells just by not stopping and not giving up.

Shake it off and take a step up!

Here's how to keep your youthful look and spirit as told by J.V.Cerney who says people's age goes fast when they permit themselves to be bogged down by worry, distrust, doubt and fear. When they lose their sense of humour they are old. Age is a state of mind. You are young as your self-confidence and your hopes for the future. You are as young as your faith and your belief, courtesy and your respect for others. You are as young as your capacity to see and to love that which is cheerful, clean, grand and beautiful. As long as your mind continues to send these messages of youth to the body there will not be ageing. There will always be youth burning on the hearth of your soul even when there is snow on the roof above.

As long as heart and soul are stimulated by that which is wholesome, and as long as people continue to act and react to that which is good, there will be no ageing. There is no ageing until you close the doors of your mind and lose self-control. There is no ageing until you lose your zest for living, when you lose that ability to accept; challenges or that spirit of adventure is vital to tomorrow. When you've lost all this you are dead.

If given a chance, all of us would desire to stay young and never want to grow old at all. When we are young, we want to grow old, but when we grow up we repent and wonder why on earth we grow old at all. When I was young I observed my dad taking decisions and having his say in many things. Even when it came to food he was the first to be given priority by my mother. At that time I felt I should grow up fast.

Today I am a father having a son. I fondly recollect my childhood days. If given a chance I wish to bounce back to my younger days. Alas! The river Ganges or the Volga cannot flow back nor can we roll back to our childhood days. Staying young means that we must not grow old as far as our looks are concerned.

THE BEST IS YET TO BE

You may come across people who make a statement saying 'I am old.' This only shows the condition of their mind. A person can grow old in age but yet he can be spiritually young. Hope for the best.

◆◆◆

21

THOUGHT IS ANOTHER NAME FOR FATE

Your life is what your thoughts are, so we have to think positive and get onto the road to success. Do not believe in luck. The moment you work sincerely and do what you should do and refrain from what you should not be doing then things will move smoothly and will join the galaxy of stars. It is here that people will call you lucky.

If you actually study successful people and also people who are happy, you will find one thing in common in them and that is their positive outlook in life. I appreciate one important point in these people and that is their positive thinking. The one question that was worrying me for a very long time is why do some people think positive and many people think negative? Is it because positive thinkers hate to think negative or is that because negative thinkers hate to think positive? It is still very difficult for one to get answers to this question.

I have been meeting a lot of people, questioning them, reading biographies and also listening to people in order to get ideas for what I am writing now. During this process I got to know several things, one important thing is the way we think, depends on two factors and that is our genes and our conditioning. This conditioning happens when we are in the womb. It is believed, if a mother carrying her baby engages in weeping, the child she gives birth too will always keep weeping. This is what was told by a speaker in a seminar that I attended. A reputed doctor who I often interact endorsed this view. Another factor is if a pregnant woman engages in laughter and positive work, she will probably give birth to a child with positive attributes. This also was endorsed by my doctor friends.

However, there is good news for people who think negatively. However negative their mothers had been when they were carrying such people, still such people can swap their thinking and think more positively and have a brighter side of life. This is a process, is not that easy, but with a little bit of mindpower one can surely make it happen.

Then comes the next important thing on thoughts. When you 'think good' all good will happen to you. At the same time when you 'think bad' all bad things will occur in your life. Keeping this in mind make it a point to entertain only 'good thoughts.' Good thoughts are like good guests. They should be welcomed, they must be fed and honoured and encouraged to keep coming time and again. Like roses good thoughts leave a sweet smell which will bring joy in our hearts. Keep your hearts open for such good guests and also do up your house to welcome such good visitors.

At the same time keep away grouches who may influence you to their way of thinking. Discard them, avoid them and even if they do come, take up some excuse and get rid of them. Indicate to them that they are not welcome at all.

It is no use to complain of bad luck. I never knew a man who was early rising, hardworking, prudent, careful of his earnings, and strictly honest ever complained of bad luck. A good character, good habits, and iron industry are impregnable to the assaults of all the ill-luck that fools ever dreamed of.

In order to get good thoughts we must learn to meditate to keep our mind still. Only when we keep our mind still, can we hear the word of God. It is believed that when we pray, we speak to God and when we keep our mind still, God speaks to us and tells us what to do, and what not to do.

I have had this beautiful experience with my beloved Mother Mary when I was at her shrine at Velanganni last year. I was in the shrine with my dad, cousin and a close friend. My dad was at the Church with my cousin while my friend sat by my side. I sat by the sea-shore from seven to nine in the evening and was listening to Mother and heard her say so many things. I got a lot of answers from Mother about my health, well-being and prosperity. Mother has granted me all what I desired. Mother will listen to any person who seeks her help. It is not necessary that one needs to be Roman Catholic like me to seek her help. Even people from other religions will be heard.

Sometimes we pretend as if we are good externally, but we have evil thoughts inside us. That is sheer hypocrisy, we may be cheating the other person, but internally we are creating an internal combustion for ourselves. The true self of a man is not in his external appearances but in what he is in his thoughts. We know many heroes in films, who are villains in real life. But in real life they are the worst people who engage in drinking, smoking, gambling, womanising, slander, cheating and all other acts which is never done by gentlemen. People foolishly believe in them and even idolise and vote for the party or buy products that they endorse. These people have 'bad inner thoughts' and 'portray a good face.' We must not get carried away, nor be like them or else we too will die of internal combustion.

A young college student was smoking a cigarette and wanted his friends' opinion on his action.

When his friends asked him, 'Who are you imitating?'

He said, 'My favourite hero of Bollywood of whom I am a great fan.'

When such stars do all these negative things on stage, the youngsters tend to imitate them. It is high time young minds imitate the good actions done by stars and not the bad ones.

Ralph Waldo Trine says, 'Thoughts follow the law of universe. You will never tell what your thoughts will do in bringing you hate or love. For thoughts are things, and their airy wings are swifter than carrier dove. They follow the law of universe. Each thing must create its kind, and they speed over the track to bring you back. Whatever went out from your mind?'

In summing up I would like to add that a person may be born of a poor family. He must never ever presume that he will not be a millionaire or a celebrity one day. That is because being a celebrity or a millionaire is not the birthright of any caste, creed or community. Anyone can become so by sheer exhibition of good thoughts in the first place, application of the thoughts into action and moving with the right people and lastly confidence that they too can make it. No one is a born genius but geniuses are made.

STORY

Once upon a time, there was a highly successful grocer who had a wonderfully furnished shop. His business was prospering. He was quite happy that many customers regularly came to his shop for their daily requirements.

To his utter surprise and disappointment a large departmental store was constructed just in front of his shop. The grocer thought that the departmental store would drive him out of business. With great distress he approached the Master and told him that his family had owned his shop for a century and to lose it now would be his undoing, for there was nothing else he was skilled at.

The Master said: 'If you fear the owner of the departmental store, you will hate him. And hatred will be your undoing.'

'What shall I do?' asked the distraught grocer?

'Each morning walk out of your shop onto the sidewalk and bless your shop, wishing it prosperity. Then turn to face the departmental store and bless it too.'

'What? Bless my competitor and destroyer?'

'Any blessing you give him will rebound to your good. And evil you wish him will destroy you.'

After a year the grocer came to the Master to inform that he had to close down his shop as he feared.

Since he became the owner of the departmental store he had to close down his grocery shop.

We are not living in isolation. Everything is knit together in this universe. This is a scientific truth. Due to this phenomenon, we are able to see the Wimbledon match in our TV set sitting at our home in Bangalore. Every thought that we have, goes all over the place. Every feeling that we entertain, pervades the entire universe. The good thoughts that we have about a person reaches him unconsciously.

Everyone could sense the good or bad feeling of others. This is an inevitable phenomenon happening continuously in our life without our conscious knowledge. Since the grocer did not hate the owner of the departmental store but rather blessed his store, in due course, they became good friends. After sometime the grocer had become a partner in the departmental store. Since the grocer had more experience he could run the departmental store more efficiently. Ultimately the earlier owner had sold all his rights of the departmental store and left the town for good.

THOUGHT

I hold it true that thoughts are things
They're endowed with bodies and breath and wings
And that we send them forth to fill
The world with good results or ill
That which we call our secret thought
Speeds forth to earth's remotest spot
Leaving its blessing or its woes
Like tracks behind as it goes
We build our future, thought by thought
For good or evil, yet know it not
Yet so the universe was wrought
Thought is another name for fate
Choose, then, thy destiny and wait
For love brings love and hate brings hate.

THE BEST IS YET TO BE

We actually become what we think. There is nothing called fate, according to me, think like a millionaire and you land up as one. Think like a beggar and you will land up as one – I hope not. Think only good. Hope for the best.

♦♦♦

22

DON'T THINK OF PEOPLE YOU DON'T LIKE

Many of us waste our precious time in thinking about people whom we don't like. We also talk much about them. We fret and fume and waste our energies in thinking about them and also talking to other people about these people whom we don't like. It is time we stop thinking about people whom we don't like if we have to become achievers.

Man is born with different faculties, thought patterns and varied mindsets. Hence all of us have got one defect or the other. The topic that I am writing about in this chapter is to tell you not to think about people whom you don't like. The prime reason is just because we don't like someone, we will have all the negatives about this person and will engage in finding fault with that person. Hence I state that one must not waste time in thinking about the person whom you don't like. I have known people who spend hours and who speak volumes about people whom they do not like. At the same time I must admit that a person who likes someone hardly takes some time to speak well about a person whom he likes.

The first question is, 'Why don't we like people?' There could be many reasons for this. One of the main reasons is some people are irritating. Many are dominating. Several are jealous. At times we don't like a person just because he is ahead of us or he is doing well. The list can go on and on.

When we ask people why they don't like a particular person, they simply say, 'I don't like him.'

We cannot ask any further questions.

In the first place I would like to add that we have to develop an attitude wherein we must never hate anybody. That goes without saying, but yet some people would not like to listen to this advice and hence they will have their own way. I must simply say that we have to forget people whom we don't like and not waste these three things on them. They are:

1. Time
2. Energy
3. Respect

Time: Time is precious and we have to use it properly. If we cannot 'talk well' about people, the least we can do is to avoid 'talking ill' about anyone. If you look at things after you speak ill of someone, what you would have gained is nothing, but somehow you feel that your burden has been lightened temporarily.

Remember the Biblical saying, 'Don't judge others, for God will not judge you.'

No man is perfect, hence we must not judge others as we will be judged for something which according to us is right and wrong in the eyes of others.

Alternative: The time that you waste talking ill about someone can be spent judiciously so that we can think of some good for others or we can use this time to think about doing something for our own good.

Energy: We build our energies through nutrition, sleep and relaxation. If we use it for the wrong purpose, we will not be in a position to get it again. It is believed that if we do the wrong thing, we will lose more energy than gaining energy for the right thing. To cite an example, you may spend a sleepless night in travel. You tend to lose about 60 runs of your life which you can gain in eating something simple and having a bout of laughter. At the same time if you fight with someone just for a couple of minutes you will tend to lose about 180 runs almost three times what you lose in travel which is a great loss of energy.

Alternative: The energy which we spend for others can be used for doing or thinking for our own purpose. It is believed that when we do some good we tend to have more energy than doing or thinking evil.

Respect: No one likes to associate with a person who talks ill of others. People who complain have very few takers unless they are wealthy and powerful. Even if they listen, it will be because they have no other go. My friend has an aged aunt whom he used to frequent when he was studying. She would complain a lot. He was at her mercy for his educational funding and would listen to her complaints. Given a chance, my friend would completely avoid her. The only person who listened to her was her maid servant who was also at her mercy.

Alternative: The more we respect, the more our soul is respected. When we respect someone and do not get respect in return we feel sad, but it is good for our soul and our conscience as the respect goes to our soul.

Any right thinking person will not want to listen to you complaining about the other person. He will simply assume that if you sit and complain to him about another person, you can always complain about him to the others. So avoid talking ill about anyone. For that matter it is better to empty your mind as far as hatred is concerned.

I remember what the great philosopher Jiddu Krishanamurthy had to say, 'I have never been insulted in my life.' That goes to say that he has never taken any insult to his heart.

There are three enemies of personal peace. They are:

1. Regret over yesterday's mistakes,
2. Anxiety over tomorrow's problems and
3. Ingratitude for today's blessing.

One of the biggest diseases that many people have is to talk about people whom they don't like. They rewind the same story time and again. We have an aged family friend in Bangalore who likes to talk to me about her family problems. What I find in her is that she talks ill about the same person whom she does not like. She may have repeated the same story to me more than eight times and she is firm on complaining about her daughter-in-law. I know the daughter-in-law personally, not once has she ever complained about her mother-in-law.

Every time she comes out with the same story with slight modifications. I get fed up listening to her, but her husband who is a very silent person tells me that the best therapy for her is to get someone to listen to her complaints.

Always avoid these three things:

1. Curses from others
2. Complaints from others against you
3. Gossip

Curses from others: Aim to get blessings from people rather than getting curses. At times even if you do not do any evil, you will get cursed, that of course is very rare. Hence work towards getting blessings rather than curses.

Complaints from others against you: At times when you do not do any mistake, someone may complain against you. Such things should not dampen your spirits. At times complaints can be taken in the right spirit. Ensure that no one complains against you.

Gossip: Do not gossip. Gossip affects three people. One is the person who is speaking. The other is the one who is listening and the last person is being talked about. Hence avoid gossip and do not encourage it.

Always fight for these three things:

1. Your rights
2. Your people
3. Your country.

Your rights: Every human is fortunate to have his right to fight. We are different from animals, which are speechless and cannot fight for their rights as man abuses his rights and kills or tortures them for his own convenience.

Your people: There is nothing wrong if you fight for the rights of people, provided you know the depth of the problem. In the world you will find different types of people, one group who dies fighting for others. It is better we be like them.

Your country: Our country comes first where priorities are concerned, hence we have to fight for the country. It is not necessary that we join the army to fight for the country, we can fight for our country by first keeping up its dignity and proving that we are proud Indians.

To sum up, let's not have enemies in our life. If one wants to have peace of mind always, it is essential that he keeps his mind free from any such knots, as such it is not good to dislike someone and even if you do, just phase them out of your mind and try not to think of them and waste your energies. The same energy can be used either to think good of that person – which is very difficult at times, or to forget them.

By thinking of our enemies, we will hurt ourselves far more than we hurt them. Let's do something constructive in life, instead of talking ill. Let's praise people so that we will get praised. Let's never waste a minute thinking about people we don't like.

STORY

The upper house of the Congress was a battle ground of heated arguments for both the Senators – Benjamin and Seward. Once like always, in the upper house of Congress, Senator Benjamin was engaged in a personal attack on Seward. It lasted for some considerable time. Then, Benjamin resumed his seat, angry and bitter, to await for a counter attack.

But what he heard just left him amazed and a little while later, Seward was seen joking with his colleagues, puffing contently on the cigar given by Benjamin.

Senator Seward sauntered up to his opponent and in his most disarming manner said – "Benjamin, give me a cigar. When your speech has been printed, send me two copies."

Message

You have the choice to either forget the people whom you don't like or react like the way Seward did in this story.

THE BEST IS YET TO BE

We waste a lot of time in carrying tales about people whom we don't like. Stop that right now and think something else which will keep you in good humour. Change your thinking. If you are in bad times, good times will come hope for the best.

◆◆◆

23

MISTAKES, A PART OF OUR LIVES

Great mistakes have led to inventions and discoveries. If we are enjoying privileges in life today it is because of the great mistakes that were done by our fore-fathers in several areas. An example is the food that we eat. Many experiments would have been done to taste and test food. Hence I state that mistakes are a part and parcel of life. We have to do mistakes to learn.

No human does a mistake deliberately, and for that matter even if a person commits a mistake, he does it unconsciously and most often mistakes are done by children. When children do mistakes it is a learning step for them. When adults commit a mistake, they do it without any intentions or there are a very few people who commit mistakes deliberately just to take some revenge or punish others.

It is not a crime to make a mistake as we are all humans and 'to err is human'. But the tragedy is, many people make mistakes deliberately or do it purposefully to hurt others or to prove the other person wrong. This is wrong on anybody's part. Another factor is when we know we are making mistakes, we have to identify and ensure that we do not repeat the same mistakes again.

Fortunately we know what to eat and what not to eat, that is because it has taken ages for man to know what is edible and what is not edible. When people make mistakes we blame them. Do you know some 90% of the people who make mistakes do it unintentionally? Only 10% of the people do it intentionally.

I did a lot of mistakes in my life. I began by working on a sewing machine where I broke needles. The next was I took the cycle to learn riding and hurt myself damaging many parts of the cycle. I learnt cycling in the bargain. I did several mistakes like this. The most important factor that one must learn is that he must not repeat mistakes once he knows that they are wrong. Many people continue to do mistakes in spite of knowing that it is a mistake. We all must learn from our mistakes and try to climb up the ladder of success.

In 1914 Thomas Alva Edison's factory in West Orange, New Jersey, was virtually destroyed by fire. Although the damage exceeded $2 million, the buildings were insured for only $238,000 because they were made of concrete and were thought to be fireproof. Much of Edison's life work went up in smoke and flames that December night. At the height of the fire, Edison's 24-year-old son, Charles, searched frantically for his father. He finally found him, calmly watching the fire, his face glowing in the reflection, his white hair blowing in the wind.

'My heart ached for him,' said Charles.
'He was 67- no longer a young man - and everything was going up in flames.
When he saw me, he shouted, 'Charles, where's your mother?'
When I told him I didn't know, he said, 'Find her. Bring her here. She will never see anything like this as long as she lives.''

The next morning, Edison looked at the ruins and said, 'There is great value in disaster. All our mistakes are burned up. Thank God we can start anew.'

If such a thing takes place in India, either it will be to claim insurance, or we will blame others for the disasters, we have quite a lot of lessons to learn from Europeans.

We must not try to find fault with others as we ourselves are vulnerable to mistakes.

Here's a small story to illustrate the fact.

A mother and son were washing dishes while the father and daughter were watching television. Suddenly, there was a crash of breaking dishes, then complete silence.

The girl looked at her father and said. 'It was mum.' 'How do you know?' The girl replied. 'Mum did not say anything,' said the girl.

Some people are adept at finding fault with others but never realise that they too commit mistakes at times. To err is human. As we err let us learn to forgive the mistakes of others.

THOUGHT

A man, who has committed a mistake and doesn't correct it, is committing another mistake.

Everything has beauty, but not everyone sees it.

Always and in everything let there be reverence.

If you know, to recognise that you know, if you don't know, to realise that you don't know: That is knowledge.

Never hesitate to ask a lesser person.

Never seek illicit wealth.

People with virtue must speak out; People who speak are not all virtuous.

What you do not wish upon yourself, extend not to others.

We take great pains to persuade others that we are happy than in endeavouring to think so ourselves.

Better a diamond with a flaw than a pebble without.

In-a-lighter-vein

If a barber makes a mistake,
It's a new style.

If a driver makes a mistake,
It's an accident.

If a doctor makes a mistake,
it's an operation.

If an engineer makes a mistake,
it's a new venture.

If parents make a mistake,
it's a new generation.

If a politician makes a mistake,
It's a new law.

If a scientist makes a mistake,
It's a new invention.

If a teacher makes a mistake,
It's a new theory.

If our boss makes a mistake,
It is our mistake...

If an employee makes a mistake,
It's a 'MISTAKE'

We must accept our mistakes gracefully. Here's what Dr Samuel Johnson did when he brought out a dictionary which was very well received by the public as well as the critics. To commemorate the success of the publication a grand dinner party was arranged for Dr. Johnson. During the party everybody praised the quality and contents of the dictionary.

Dr. Johnson too charmed everyone present there with his intellectual talk about his latest work. While everybody was praising the dictionary one old lady who interrupted and expressed her astonishment at the fact that an error was noticed by her in the great scholar's work. Further she pointed out the exact mistake in the dictionary. Everyone present there was shocked beyond words. They were anxiously waiting for the reply of Dr. Johnson.

Dr. Johnson coolly replied: 'Ignorance madam, pure ignorance, kindly accept my humble apology.'

Dr. Johnson is a great scholar well-known for his literary work. His humility is admirable. The first test of a really great man is his humility. Humility does not indicate the quality of doubting one's own ability but acknowledges that what is known is very little but what is yet to be learnt is immeasurable.

Commit mistakes and learn many things - that I do not like these cold, precise, perfect people, who in order not to speak wrong, never speak at all and in order not to do wrong, never do anything.

It is not at all necessary that every attempt should end in a conspicuous success. Even great people have made mistakes and have then come up in life. You can also feel discouraged by the fact that you do not seem to be achieving your aim. That your aim itself may be too high for your present powers will not occur to you, for after all we all have exaggerated notion of our own powers. At the age of eighteen, for example you are not expected to write a novel like Jeffry Archer, although it is more than likely that you may not try to do so. If you have the genius for the piano, as had Richard Clayderman, nobody expects you to produce a fine violin concert. You need to recognise the type of ability you possess, and also how far that ability extends. There is no harm in experimenting with various things, you are likely to make mistakes. But lack of achievement should not cause you to feel inferior and incapable. At such a moment, remind yourself that what you are doing is for your pleasure; whether you produce something worthwhile at the end of your labour or not, all things said and done.

Making mistakes is a very common phenomenon, it depends on the degree of mistakes that one does. If an Air Traffic Controller makes a mistakes, that can lead to an air disaster where several lives will be lost, but if a tailor makes a mistake, he can set it right or for that matter if a cobbler makes a mistake, he is likely to mend it.

Thomas Edison lived to be 84 years young and patented an impressive 1093 inventions. Although he did not always work alone, that's still impressive. Considering his first invention was at the age of 22 in the year 1869, what was impressive is he did a lot of mistakes and learnt a lot of lessons from them.

When his friend asked him one day, 'When are going to retire?'

He said, 'I am not satisfied with what I have done, I am waiting for the best to come.'

When children make a mistake they get frightened of their parents. Many children have fled their homes fearing their parents. Some have returned and some have not. When I was young I stealthily took my fathers scooter and began driving it, when the fuel got over, we dumped the scooter and went away to my friend's house. My father almost lodged a police complaint when his friend told him that the scooter was lying on the road. He took it and came home, but he did not suspect me.

Today my son who is five-year-old tries his hand at drawing and draws on the wall, my wife shouts at him but I keep quiet. I do not want to curtail his creativity, lest he gets dejected in life. On one occasion he had written a b c d on my personal room wall. My wife told him that he would get a beating from me. He feared the worst when I went to Bangalore. I smiled at him and he hugged me. He began rubbing it himself. He writes very neatly now.

THE BEST IS YET TO BE

When you do a mistake and get a battering, do not give up, mistakes lead to inventions, discoveries and good thoughts, it can also change your thoughts and make you better in life. Hope for the best.

◆◆◆

24

RELATIONSHIP – VISA TO A NEAR ONE

Thought - when you miss someone, you get over to them to know that you are thinking of them. But the truth is you want them to know you are thinking about them. Only man among God's creatures know the value of relationship and hence he must keep it up, lest we join the band of animals and birds who know nothing about relationship.

Man is the only living being that believes in relationship. Even other animals and birds do, but for a very short period of time. The birds look after the young ones, after some time the young ones fly away. Same is the case with animals too, where either man separates them or they leave on their own. Relationship is a very powerful word which has to be nurtured through toil, understanding and love. Unless there is love there won't be good relationship.

Relationship is very important in this world. Especially in human relationships. Relationship breaks due to three reasons. They are:

1. Ego
2. Money Matters
3. Property Disputes.

Ego: Man is born with different ego states and hence if he is not treated properly he tends to dislike a person and may even go to the extent of breaking the relationship.

Money Matters: This is a very common factor when money matters come in, then relationship tends to break. When a person gives money to his relative or a friend, he must keep in mind he is taking a risk on relationship. So far as the money is paid on time, it is all right, but if the money does not go back to the person who has given it, the relationship is strained.

Today people are so obsessed with money that they tend to throw all norms to the winds for money. I have known brothers fighting and not seeing each others faces due to money problems. Most often problems in money matters arise not out of one's own money but money left behind by ancestors to be shared equally.

Property Disputes: This is one other reason why relationships break. Own brothers take each other to the court. It is relatives who fight it out in courts and in the open just for the sake of property which they don't realise they will not carry with them when they go to the grave.

There is another factor also which is responsible for breaking relationship and that is I have observed and studied some people, some in my family too. They have a peculiar habit of hating people. Some also do not love people and want to stay aloof. They do not value human relationship and hate to be in the midst of people. There are very few people in this category who actually hate people, probably they are born with such traits which makes them behave in this manner. There is very little that we can do to bring these type of people to track.

Certain families have developed cracked relationships over a period of years and it is carried forward by the younger generations. My father had a problem with his two bothers over some issue. He left his parents and two brothers immediately after marriage. We were grown up with the patronage and help from our mother's family. We would meet our cousins and elders from my fathers side but we could not see each others' faces. This went on for several years while each one started realising that keeping away from the other was of no use.

I was the first to break the barrier much against the wishes of some of my relatives. When they realised that I was determined they did not bother. My aunts and cousins had some reservation interacting with me but when they saw the purpose behind my coming to them they welcomed me and today I play a very important role in my family affairs. I have also trained the younger generations to be united and not follow what our elders did in the past.

Relationships can be of seven types. Each one plays an important role in our lives and we have to give each one their space. They are:

1. Grandparents
2. Parents
3. Spouses
4. Children
5. Nephews & Nieces
6. Uncles and Aunts
7. Relatives

Grandparents: If you have grandparents or a parent, frequent them and seek their blessings. Try to spend time with them, stay with them and get to know many things that occurred in the past. They are the best persons with wisdom. Make them feel important.

Parents: Parents are next to God. We have to worship them. We also have to give them respect not just because they look after us but it is our moral duty to do so. We have to look after them till their last days. They must be given even more importance than our spouses.

Spouses: One must have a very good relationship with their spouses. Spouses must be given their space but not at the cost of our parents and elders. However a wife when she enters her in-laws house must embrace her in-laws like her own parents. The husband on the other side must also respect his in-laws like his own parents.

Children: Parents must respect their children, love them and guide them and not abuse or snub them for any reason. Children must not be pampered. When parents love children, they will do the same when they grow up especially when parents depend on their children.

Nephews & Nieces: Our nephews and nieces also play an important role in our lives. We have to nurture them and love them. We also have to guide and help them in their needs, be it emotional, financial or moral. We must give them extra care if they do not have a parent. However, they must not be pampered.

Uncles and Aunts: Most uncles and aunts play an indirect role in our up-bringing. I grew up in a joint family and most of the time I would hang around in my aunt's place. They looked after me equally like their own children. We have to give them their due.

Relatives: Relatives must be given importance as they are the ones who come handy in events that are good and bad. Relatives are the first to arrive when there is a marriage or a funeral in the family. Hence we have to have good relationship with all of them.

God gives us relatives, thank God we can choose our friends. We have the options to continue our relationship with our relatives, we also have the choice to decide on friends.

No man is an island. He needs relationships, especially the seven ones that are mentioned above. It depends on each person as to how he wants to maintain relationship with each of the categories that are given. It depends on each one's taste and the way in which one finds the other one important in his life to maintain a relationship.

The man who has not had all these people to live with would have never lived a life. When I say relationship, I mean it is emotional and physical. Whereas physical relationship exists between spouses, emotional relationship can exist between all the seven categories I have mentioned.

Recently a friend of mine who has travelled to several countries met me. We were at a dinner party. I asked him how many countries he had travelled. He was blushing when he said about six countries including America, England, France, Germany, Canada and Russia. Then I asked him a question which took him some time to answer.

I asked him, 'How difficult it is to get a visa to go to these countries?'

He said, 'It is quite easy except the United States of America and United Kingdom.'

I then went on to ask him, 'You got a visa to go far away and travel 5000 miles, but you have still not applied for a visa to travel 5 kilometres to visit your father's only sister who lives in Bangalore?'

He was silent. After some time he paused, took a drink and said, 'What should I do, I need permission from my people to do so.'

I asked, 'What? Permission to visit a dear one?'

Then I told him the story of how I had broken the barrier by meeting my relatives much against my family members' orders.

We discussed a lot that night and he became emotional. I got his aunt on the phone and got my friend to speak to her. He wept, she too wept and it was such a wonderful experience for both. I fixed a meeting early the next day over breakfast. We went there. My friend's aunt hugged him and she took me also in her arms and said:

'You are also one of my nephews from today for the wonderful service you have done.'

I was happy that I could help build relationship with someone. I swear I do not have a single enemy in my life, even if there is one, he or she may assume I am an enemy for him or her but I surely do not harbour any hatred that is what I call relationship.

St Augustine of Hippo beautifully says: 'Forgive from your heart. There are many kinds of alms, the giving of which helps us to obtain pardon for our sins; but none is greater than the one by which we forgive from our heart a sin that some one has committed against us.'

Take the example of a politician. He must be a master in building relationships with the members of his constituency. If he has a bad reputation or he does not have good relationship with the local people, he will be shown the door in the next election. Relationship is not just for politicians but for all human beings who live on this earth.

STORY

A king once underestimated his people and had very bad relations with the people. There came a day when he went into the forests and had a tough time as a pride of lions chased his entourage. The soldiers got scattered and the king was lying wounded. Many people who went to the forest to collect wood noticed him, but refused to give him any medication as he had very bad relationship with the people of his kingdom. Back home also he ill-treated his wife and snubbed his subjects. There was not a single person with whom the king had good relationship with. His physician also was waiting for an opportunity to run away from the kingdom.

The king who was badly injured and lying unconscious was however saved by some broad-minded people who said that he had already learnt his lesson. His soldiers could have saved him, but they were more interested in saving their chief and also saving their own lives. When he came back he realised the importance of relationship and apologised to the people.

THE BEST IS YET TO BE

When you have a problem in relationship and someone is snubbing you, don't worry as good times will come to you. Remember the people who are ignoring your relationship will one day come to you and ask you to be good to them. Hope for the best.

◆◆◆

25

ENCOURAGE YOURSELF

Even if the whole world is against you, you can still do wonders and marvels by encouraging yourself. When you encourage yourself, you can do anything. All persons who have achieved something great in life have been encouraging themselves. Encourage yourself even at odd times, even if you feel you are in the last stage of life.

Encouragement is something that drives man to do great things in life, it also serves as a solace for many a wounded heart. Encouragement is one thing that a person can do, another important factor is self-encouragement which is even more important than encouragement alone.

Encouragement can come from three sources. They are:

1. Self Encouragement
2. Encouragement from others
3. Encouragement from seeing something.

Self Encouragement: Most often we are called to encourage ourselves especially when it comes to a failure or when something goes wrong. There are a very small percentage of people who do what we call self-encouragement.

Percentage quoted is as follows – 15%

Encouragement from others: Very often we see parents, elders and relatives including our teachers encouraging us in life. Most often it is the parents who encourage their children. We also have several cases where friends encourage us to do several things, sometimes even the bad ones.

Percentage quoted is as follows – 60%

Encouragement from seeing something: At times we do not encourage our self, neither does anyone encourage us. It is during this time that we encourage ourselves after we either meet a person or see something happening.

Percentage quoted is as follows – 25%

Several people fail in life due to lack of this rare quality. That is not being encouraged by others. What I state here is, 'Why wait for someone to encourage you, do it yourself.' It is not necessary for someone to push you, if you wait for that push, you will land up nowhere.

I wish to narrate a small tale in this context. I was in Kolkata to attend a conference sometime ago. I had the privilege to meet an erudite person. He took me home and showed his personal library. Almost all the categories of books were present there. Most of the books were all bundled and kept there. He also had very good knowledge. I learnt that he was financially not sound and depended on people to give him money to have his food. He was a bachelor and never married. I discussed with him his state of affairs while having dinner.

He said, 'I received no encouragement from my parents, elders and friends and hence I could not forge ahead in life.'

I understood that he had several mental blocks and had failed in life. When I told him that I too had received no encouragement but only discouragement, snubbing and negative remarks, but still I managed to forge ahead in life.

He simply said, 'All five fingers are not the same.'

I then came to a conclusion that he had a firm mindset and that one must change and not wait for encouragement by others.

Even a fallen man can rise only if he has the will to do so. The whole world may encourage you to get up, but if you wish not to get up you will still be there. But even if the whole world says that you can't get up and just you alone think that you can do it, you will rise against all odds. That is the way in which you can encourage yourself in doing so.

This is something which we all must do for ourselves. Even if the whole world is against us, we can still come out successfully in our lives. There can be nothing better than encouraging ourselves into doing something.

Before you encourage yourself you must make friendship with yourself. There are a lot of people in this world who hate themselves for several reasons. Most of the people who commit suicide hate themselves. Most meditation teachers recommend beginning by using some simple object as an aid, but the important thing to remember is that it is not the particular object or technique that matters. What's important is the process of bringing one's mind back to its object of focus when it wanders. It's important to do this gently and without judgement by the way. Meditation takes effort, but it is not a war. It is a way of making friends with yourself.

A friend of the great inventor Thomas Alva Edison once dropped in to his house and said that Edison had failed miserably and he still continued to work on his inventions.

Thomas Edison said that it was not 'failures' but they were 'attempts.'

All along he kept encouraging himself.

Speak only encouraging words to yourself even if you have a setback. When you are down and out, all you have to do is to say some encouraging words. I have been doing it in my dark days. I got this from a book by Dale Carnegie. That statement in the book also impressed me about him saying, 'When you are down and out, think of good times to come.'

Edgar Guest says, 'Do the things that others may think it can't be done. Somebody said that it couldn't be done. But he with a chuckle replied that 'may be it couldn't' but he would be one who wouldn't say so till he'd tried. So he buckled right in with the trace of a grin on his face. If he worried he hid it. He started to sing as he tackled the thing that couldn't be done, and he did it.'

One day a friend of mine came to my flat and was sitting in my office room. What he saw was the picture of a car, a poster with billions of dollars, an expensive watch worn by a model and many motivational things. My business was dull; he made fun of me and said all these things were a waste. I just smiled and after he went I was sad at what he said. I then encouraged myself and went on.

Today I don't meet the same friend, he is down and out. All that I visualized and pasted on the wall are mine, except for the billions of dollars which I don't have, but I may have them in due course. I am confident about it.

Write down a positive statement and take that sheet of paper and keep in it in your wallet and keep looking at it time and again. When someone writes something special about you, take that and keep looking at it and you will find a great change in your life.

Another important thing that you must do is to always talk good about a person even if he has defects. Remember every man has got some good in him. At times what we see as bad may be good where he is concerned. I recently met a butcher who kills goats mercilessly.

When I asked him if he was not feeling guilty, he simply said, 'No, I help people eat good non-vegetarian food.'

He was right according to himself.

Keep a set of currency notes (denominations of One Thousand, Five Hundred, One Hundred, Fifty, Twenty, Ten, Five, Two and One) in your wallet and feel it at least thrice a day. You can consider having a Dollar and Pound sterling too along with a Euro. Keep looking at it every day and open them up and feel it and put it back in its place. By doing this you are encouraging yourself to have more money in your life. When you do this with confidence you gain more money, but then again money will not come if you do not make plans to earn it, wish for it and pep it up with action, it will come.

If you study the lives of great men and those who have achieved success. Most of them have encouraged themselves in all forms. Such people not only encourage themselves but they also encourage others. A very typical example is our teachers and lecturers who teach us daily. What they do constantly is the conditioning which is equivalent to encouraging us to achieve certain goals and aims in life. Another example is if you happen to attend a training programme the trainer constantly encourages the participants to proceed towards their goals in life.

THOUGHT

When you have lost everything, you still have something.
That is not wealth or anything else.
You still have something and that is your own encouragement.

STORY

The Philistine army had gathered for war against Israel. The two armies faced each other, camped for battle on opposite sides of a steep valley. A Philistine giant measuring over nine feet tall and wearing full armour came out each day for forty days, mocking and challenging the Israelites to fight. His name was Goliath. Saul, the King of Israel, and the whole army were terrified of Goliath.

One day David, the youngest son of Jesse, was sent to the battle lines by his father to bring back news of his brothers. David was probably just a young teenager at the time. While there, David heard Goliath shouting his daily defiance and he saw the great fear stirred within the men of Israel. David responded, 'Who is this uncircumcised Philistine that he should defy the armies of God?'

So David volunteered to fight Goliath. It took some persuasion, but King Saul finally agreed to let David fight against the giant. Dressed in his simple tunic, carrying his shepherd's staff, slingshot and a pouch full of stones, David approached Goliath. The giant cursed at him, hurling threats and insults.

David said to the Philistine, 'You come against me with sword and spear and javelin, but I come against you in the name of the Lord Almighty, the God of the armies of Israel, whom you have defied ... today I will give the carcasses of the Philistine army to the birds of the air ... and the whole world will know that there is a God in Israel ... it is not by sword or spear that the Lord saves; for the battle is the Lord's, and He will give all of you into our hands.'

As Goliath moved in for the kill, David reached into his bag and slung one of his stones at Goliath's head. Finding a hole in the armour, the stone sank into the giant's forehead and he fell face down on the ground. David then took Goliath's sword killed him and then cut off his head. When the Philistines saw that their hero was dead, they turned and ran. So the Israelites pursued, chasing and killing them and plundering their camp.

What David did was he encouraged himself and said that he 'would do it.'

THE BEST IS YET TO BE

The one and only thing which according to me keeps company with you when you are in trouble and when you are in dark days is encouraging yourself. When you do this be sure that good days are there for you. Hope for the best.

◆◆◆

26

ATTITUDE IS EVERYTHING

A person's attitude in life actually determines the altitude he will go. Most often people fail to make it because of the wrong attitude. Even if we are born with negative attitudes, we can still turn them in our favour if we look at people with positive attitudes and change.

If you look at the persons who are successful and those who are not, you will find one thing in common and that is; the person who is successful will have a better and positive attitude towards life than others. At the same time, the ones who are not successful will surely have a problem with their attitude.

I can only tell you one simple truth from my own experience and that of others whom I have known closely and that is 'if your attitude is right, everything will be right, that is even if others are wrong; but if something is wrong with your attitude, even if the others are right, you will feel they are wrong.'

Why are some people having a good attitude while several others have bad attitudes. We actually do not know the reason but the way in which we conduct ourselves is largely due to four factors. They are:

1. Hereditary factors
2. Circumstances
3. Influences
4. Bottom-line

Hereditary: We are born with the traits of our parents and ancestors. We tend to behave like them. But these things can be modified with our consent.

Circumstances: At times we are forced to do certain things that we cannot do, but we do it out of compulsion, fear and obligation. Attitude can also change here.

Influences: We may live in an opulent home or may reside in a slum. We do what we have to do in these places. While the behaviour of a person residing in a mansion is totally different from that of a person who dwells in a slum.

Bottom-line: The bottom line is whatever may be your attitude, you can very well decide to change it for the better. It is a little difficult to change over immediately but with constant practice, determination and struggle you can do anything in this world. Attitude is very important for the growth of all human beings.

Developing a positive attitude adds to our quality of life and spreads like wildfire to others. At times our positive attitude can enhance the quality lives of others too.

STORY

An old man lived alone in Minnesota. He wanted to spade his potato garden, but it was very hard work. His only son, who would have helped him, was in prison. The old man wrote a letter to his son and mentioned his situation:

Dear Son, I am feeling pretty bad because it looks like I won't be able to plant my potato garden this year. I hate to misdo the garden, because your mother always loved planting time. I'm just getting too old to be digging up a garden plot. If you were here, all my troubles would be over. I know you would dig the plot, for me if you weren't in the prison. Love, Dad

Shortly, the old man received this telegram: 'For Heaven's sake, Dad, don't dig up the garden. That's where I buried the guns.' At 4 a.m. the next morning, a dozen FBI agents and local police officers showed up and dug up the entire garden without finding any guns. Confused, the old man wrote another note to his son telling him what happened and asked him what to do next.

His son's reply was: 'Go ahead and plant your potatoes, Dad it's the best I could do for you from here.'

No matter where you are in the world, if you have decided to do something deep from your heart, you can do it; it is the thought that matters not where you are.

A certain master put a wooden bird atop a pole and asked three disciples to shoot the bird.
While the first person aimed for the bird, he missed it by an inch.
The second person aimed for the bird and missed it by a couple of inches.
The third man took a deep breath; he aimed for the bird's eye and brought it down.
The master immediately came to a conclusion that the third person had more focus than the other two.

These are the seven steps for staying positive in a negative world:

They are:

1. Understanding
2. Learner
3. Reading
4. Self-improvement
5. Motivation
6. Inspiration
7. Positives

Understanding: Understand that failure is an event, it is not a person. Yesterday ended last night; today is a brand new day, and it's yours. You were born to win, but to be a winner you must plan to win, prepare to win, and then you can expect to win.

Learner: Become a lifetime learner. Learn just one new word every day and in five years you will be able to talk with just about anybody about anything. When your vocabulary improves, your I.Q. goes up 100% of the time.

Reading: Read something useful, informational or inspirational every day. Look up the dictionary and thesaurus. Read a passage and write it down and pronounce words audibly, it will improve your language and also your intelligence.

Self-improvement: Listen to motivational CDs and also attend seminars and lectures by eminent speakers. Read a lot of self-improvement books.

Motivation: Start the day by stating 'I resolve to be happy today'. Smile and laugh. Read inspirational messages every day. Begin and end the day by reading or doing something positive.

Inspiration: The best way to remain happy is to take whatever comes your way positively, do not bother about small irritants.

Positives: Remember, success is a process, not an event. Invest the time in building a positive attitude. It will pay off well in your skills as well as your career.

I have known one thing that is true. If you have the right attitude and the entire world is against you, you still have a fair chance of doing well in life. At the same time if you have a bad attitude and the whole world is in your favour, you may be in their favour for a short while, soon you will fall from grace. Hence if you have a positive attitude, you will shine in life.

Attitude is everything

There once was a woman who woke up one morning, looked

in the mirror, and noticed she had only three strands of hairs on her head.

'Well,' she said, 'I think I'll braid my hair today?' So she did and she had a wonderful day.

The next day she woke up, looked in the mirror and saw that she had only two strands of hairs on her head.

'H-M-M,' she said, 'I think I'll part my hair down the middle today?' So she did and she had a grand day.

The next day she woke up, looked in the mirror and noticed that she had only one strand of hair on her head.

'Well,' she said, 'Today I'm going to wear my hair in a pony tail.' So she did and she had a funny day.

The next day she woke up, looked in the mirror and noticed that there wasn't a single strand of hair on her head.

'Yea!' she exclaimed, 'I don't have to fix my hair today!'

Attitude is everything.

Be kinder than necessary, to everyone you meet is fighting some kind of battle.

Live simply,
Love generously,
Care deeply,
Speak kindly.......

Positive Attitude

If you think you are beaten you are;
If you think you dare not, you don't;

If you want to win but think you can't;
it's almost a cinch you won't.

If you think you'll lose you're lost;
for out of the world we find

Success begins with a fellow's will;
it's all in a state of mind.

Life's battles don't always go
to the stronger and faster man,

But sooner or later the man who wins
is the man who thinks he can.

A study attributed to Harvard University found that when a person gets a job 85% of the time it is because of his attitude, and only 15% of the time because of how smart they are and how many facts and figures they know. Surprisingly, almost 100% of our present day education goes to teach facts and figures which account for only 15% of success in work.

Just like an absence of ill health does not equal good health, an absence of negativity alone does not make a person positive. People with positive attitudes have certain personality traits that are easy to recognise. They are caring, confident, patient, and humble. They have high expectations of themselves and others. They anticipate positive outcomes. A person with a positive attitude is like a fruit of all seasons. He is always welcome.

We need to become good finders. We need to focus on the positive in life. Let's not start looking for what is wrong. Because of our conditioning, we are so attuned to finding fault and looking for what is wrong that we forget to see the positive picture.

Even in Heaven, fault finders will find faults. Most people find what they are looking for. If they are looking for friendship, happiness and the positive, that is what they get. If they are looking for fights or indifference, then that is what they get, and yes, looking for the positive does not mean over looking faults.

Count your blessings, not your troubles. Take time to smell the roses. When I say count your blessings, it is just the positive things. Many people sit and count their troubles. After all one must understand the joy of thinking positive and being positive has definitely got more advantages than negatives in life.

Unfortunately I have come across certain people who behave in a very peculiar way. They have a serious problem with their attitude. Probably they may have been born with such traits. But when we tell them they do not listen to us. They take things in a wrong sense.

A friend of mine once said, 'When there is a problem with a person's attitude, we just can't do anything.'

But I disagree with my friend as I am a living example. I had a very negative attitude as a child. When people corrected me I have taken it positively and thankfully I am in a position to speak to people about attitude. It is a choice between a person who desires success and one who does not want to be successful. Some people want to stick to their conviction and remain where they are, stagnating in life.

You can bring about certain changes in your attitude if you want to have an edge over the others in life and that is as easy as your consent to do so.

THE BEST IS YET TO BE

When you have a good or a positive attitude and the whole world is against you, you still have hope that the world will acknowledge you; it is just a matter of time for people to recognise you and your ability. Hope for the best.

♦♦♦

27

CREATE A HEAVEN WITHIN YOU

Heaven is a place where people who were good on earth reside. When we live in joy and peace we claim it is like Heaven or paradise. Heaven according to the Bible is above us and Hell is below us. Many believe that it is a state of mind and not a physical place. Hence when it comes to living, we can make a Heaven of our lives.

Of late I have been living with a very strong and positive statement which I got from one of my spiritual masters - the great Osho. 'Your mind can be a healer or it can even be a killer, it depends on how you control your mind.' It is like a truck which is in the driver's hand. The driver can take it at any speed he wants to. He can go slow, he can go fast, he can even bang up another vehicle or he can even take it down into a lake or a river. Hence we have to condition our mind in such a way that it brings us just joy, peace and happiness and nothing else.

Most people I have seen talk about the Heaven that is above us where God is seated. No one knows if such a physical place ever exists or not. Some even believe that Heaven exists but it a state of mind and can be stretched into a physical place where the imaginative mind is concerned. However what I am here to tell you is we can make our lives happy, we can also make others happy and we ourselves can be responsible for making the lives of others happy. When we do this, we are making a Heaven for the others and also for our own selves.

Well, all said and done, Heaven exists unmindful of the location, it is there and enough evidence is there to prove that God is in heaven and He controls the universe from there. But no one has come back to state how Heaven looks or who resides there except for some great Saints who have shared their experiences about heaven.

I spoke to seven people and asked them how their life was, and if it was like Heaven or if it was like being in hell or mediocre. Here's what they had to say. They are:

1. Always Heaven
2. Forever Hell
3. Mediocre
4. Majority Heaven Minority Hell
5. Majority Hell and Minority Heaven
6. Fifty-Fifty Hell and Heaven
7. Depends, sometimes Heaven, at times Hell.

Always Heaven: This category of people took life positively and said that they enjoyed life. Heaven was on earth for them. They felt that there was a better 'Heaven' above the earth which was governed by 'God'.

Forever Hell: This group of people felt life was a misery and that they suffered at the hands of people. They even went to the extent of telling me that 'God' had only created them, but 'Satan' had taken control of their lives.

Mediocre: This cluster of people whom I met said at times it was 'rain' and at times it was 'sunshine'. They said everything that occurred was a part of life. At times we felt 'miserable' and at times we felt 'encouraged'.

Majority Heaven Minority Hell: These people felt 'most of the time it was Heaven' while even hell haunted. They argue how Satan could be sitting quiet when the kingdom of God reigns; hence we have a 'little bit of hell' too in our lives.

Majority Hell and Minority Heaven: When I spoke to this group of people they claimed that they faced 'misery most of the time'. The only time they felt nice was 'when they had no work' and when they were at rest or when they were at some function.

Fifty-Fifty Hell and Heaven: This group of people felt that it was 'balanced'. Hell was knocking at their doors as much as Heaven knocked at their doors. It was a fifty-fifty issue for them.

Depends, sometimes Heaven, at times Hell: This category of people felt that 'nothing was certain', anything could happen. It could be the good as well as the bad.

After interacting with these people I have come to a conclusion that whatever happens in our life is our own creation. We can make a hell if we want, or we can create a Heaven if we desire. That is in our hands and we can choose to do either. Any right thinking person will want to create a Heaven for him and for the others.

The two types of Heaven which I would like to talk about is a Heaven within ourselves and the Heaven outside our human body. Both the Heavens are inter-related. By this I mean, if we have a Heaven which is inside us, we will surely have much to feel happy outside where we can enjoy that Heaven too.

We have heard what Heaven is. Some people believe Heaven is a physical place where we go after we do well on earth and then reach this place and enjoy eternal life. When a place is bad, we say it is hell, we also utter the words 'Oh hell'. This, we utter when something goes wrong.

Another thing that I would like to touch upon is death. We are all afraid of death. Given a chance none of us want to die, we want to live. We don't want death. Almost all humans are afraid of death. Here's a story to illustrate the fact.

A millionaire was sitting and counting money. In life he was a terror. He never feared anybody. He was very bold and took a lot of chances to earn money and took risks in business and yet one day when the Angel of death appeared to him and asked him to get ready, he tried bribing the Angel and said that he would give ten per cent share of the wealth. The Angel did not agree, he offered it 25 per cent, yet the Angel did not agree, he then offered fifty per cent share, the Angel did not agree. He offered seventy five per cent; still the Angel did not agree and wanted him to go with it. He got fed up and said that he would give all the wealth for life. The Angel said that it was not possible. Finally he had to go with the Angel of death as he felt living without money was of no use.

For fear of death he was willing to offer all his wealth. That is what man does when he is asked to choose death; he does not want to die. Death is an opening to eternity. We all who are born must die.

The Heaven that I am about to talk about is a different one. Heaven as I told you is a place where there is peace, plenty, happiness and joy. Where there is no pain and suffering where there is no death, it is just eternal life.

In this Heaven you will find life, death, pain, suffering, good news, bad news and competition. You will find people whom you trust will pull you down, reliable people whom you trust will let you down. Sometimes spouses will cheat, at times children will beat their parents, children will also bring you misery. But in spite of all these things, you can still be happy and cross over to the final bridge with contentment.

When we make others happy, we ourselves are happy. But when we make others sad, we are also not happy. That is why we must ensure that we make others happy so that we too are happy.

Just think for a while and see how you will be when you and the others are happy, at the same time think about a situation when you are sad and you also make others sad. Sometimes you make others sad and you think you are happy, if you go deep into your subconscious mind, you also are as sad as the person who is also sad. So be happy and make others happy.

THOUGHT

Philip Doddridge says give to God each moment as it flies
Live while you live, the epicure would say
And seize the pleasures of the present day
Live while you live, the sacred preacher cries
And give to God each moment as it flies
Lord, in my views let both be united
I live in pleasure when I live to thee.

THE BEST IS YET TO BE

Heaven is a place which all cannot go to, for that matter all are not entitled to stay there. That is why we also have hell. Going to Heaven or getting down to hell strictly depends on us. Hence we have to do good deeds to reach there. The call may be late, but, hope for the best.

◆◆◆

28

BE SURE THERE'S A PROBLEM

Sometimes we tend to make a mountain out of a molehill. We create problems for ourselves. When we do this we not only bring misery to our own self but we also bring enough doom to those around us. Hence we have to verify if there is a problem at all before we assume things.

If at all we have problems in the world it is due to certain reasons and that is there are some people who are specially born to create problems. If you would have watched a tele-serial Tamas in the late eighties, a man is hired to kill a pig and throw it into a mosque only to instigate the Muslims. This is done by a group of anti-social elements just to create an ethnic conflict between the majority Hindus and minority Muslims. You all know what it can lead to.

There are also occasions where some people just to get a kick create problems in the minds of people and confuse them. I remember once when I was the chief of an express service company I had about four hundred and fifty people working under me. I was very strict with my subordinates. Once a subordinate who was not performing in the company was taken to task. He hatched a conspiracy and made a anonymous call to me threatening me with dire consequences. I took this issue to my heart. The same guy came to me and said that he had some influence in his locality. I sought his help not knowing that he was behind this episode. Soon we came to know about it and terminated his services from the company. I spent several sleepless nights, I did not stay back late in the evening, I had to take help from my colleagues to reach home. In other words my life had become miserable for about a fortnight. In the end I laughed it off that I had created problems for myself without any problem existing.

Problems have existed since ages and have not changed. It is only how we find a solution to problems. The one and unique thing with a problem is that it always comes with a solution. Most often we do not make any effort to find that solution. Problems can be of three types. They are:

1. Problem within us
2. Problem created by others for us and
3. Problems with people and things.

Problem within us: Most of us seem to be creating, exhibiting and inviting problems for ourselves. When I spoke to such people I realised that they did it unconsciously. Such people must go for counselling to get rid of this problem.

Problems created by others for us: At times we will find people creating problems for us. This they do to either take revenge on us for some reason or for the pleasure of it. These people who are victims must defend themselves.

Problems with people and things: Sometimes we have problems with people even if they don't. At times we can also have problems with things that can put us off. We have to watch out and handle such things tactfully.

This chapter is dedicated to all those who have a very clear vision of the word called 'problem' and not the other good words. I have come across such people who live with problems, feel for it, nurture it and make it a way of life. Imagine if the head of a family is such a person, what would happen to the others who are dependent on him. Some people make problems 'a mountain out of a molehill' and suffer and make others also suffer as a result of their attitude.

For some people, problems are not having money, for some people it is not owning a house. For many people it is relationship, for many it is poverty, for several it is insecurity. Some people also complain that they don't have a good job, while some people do not have a job as such. If we make a survey we will get millions of people who fall in this category.

The best way to escape from your problem is to solve it. The only important thing that one must remember is not to blow up problems as they can get worse for us and for the others for whom we create problems. It is a fact that problems are there in life and that does not mean to say we have to magnify a problem to put others in trouble. We have to find ways and means to solve them.

Most often we create problems for ourselves and suffer. We not only suffer, but we also put others in trouble. Problems are an integral part of life. Without problems life would be a lull. Once some people went to God and pleaded with Him to take away all their problems. God did what they wanted. Life became boring. The same people went to God and asked Him to bring back problems into the world. Since then man has never asked God to remove problems. Problems actually make men tough. They are like passing clouds.

When man was acting in the right manner, the world was right. There was a strict disciplinarian father. He had a brilliant daughter noted for her naughtiness. One day he was seriously doing some work and his daughter was disturbing him too much. He wanted to make her seriously engaged in a work so that he could peacefully continue his work. He took a world map from the newspaper, cut into different sizes and asked her to put it back again.

The father's intention was that the girl would take quite sometime to put the world map together. On receiving the paper the girl looked at it and then finished her job in no time. She called her father and informed him that she was able to put the world map together. The father was surprised at her dexterity and asked her how she was able to manage it.

The girl replied, 'Behind the world map, which was cut into pieces, there was the picture of a man. When the man was set right, the world map was also easily constructed.'

People make the world. Set right the man, the world will be set right. All the major problems of the world are created by man himself.

Management Lesson

One fine day, a bus driver five feet, thin and basically meek went to the bus garage, started his bus, and drove off along the route. No problems for the first few stops - a few people got on, a few got off, and things went generally well.

At the next stop, however, a big hulk of a guy got on. Six feet height, built like a wrestler, arms hanging down to the ground. He glared at the driver and said, 'Big John doesn't pay!' and sat down at the back.

Well, he was. Naturally, he didn't argue with Big John, but he wasn't happy about it. The next day the same thing happened - big John got on again, made a show of refusing to pay, and sat down. And the next day, and the next.

This grated on the bus driver, who started losing sleep over the way big John was taking advantage of him. Finally he could stand it no longer. He signed up for body building courses, karate, judo, and all that good stuff.

By the end of the summer, he had become quite strong; what's more, he felt really good about himself. So on the next

Monday, when big John once again got on the bus and said, 'Big John doesn't pay!'

The driver stood up, glared back at the passenger, And screamed, 'And why not?' With a surprised look on his face, big John replied, 'Big John has a bus pass.'

Management Moral: 'Be sure there is a problem in the first place before working hard to solve one.' Culingigon and Sedlack say, 'When problems mount do something, no matter what? When problems mount, and death, divorce, illness, job loss, and other problems seem to threaten our sanity, balance, and health, do something. Do anything but don't sit and moan. Walk, jog, swim, soak in a tub, take a sauna, see a movie, flirt, make love, eat, read, argue, telephone your friends, and talk. Talk in itself is therapeutic. Cry if you can, but keep moving physically, emotionally and spiritually. Try to realise that through all these adversities we learn and grow. See if you can discern what the lessons are in trying circumstances.'

Before we come to a conclusion, we have to first confirm if the problem exists, only then we have to react or find a solution. We must not fume and lose our head and go mad and make others also mad without knowing the actual facts. One has to have his head over his shoulders when he takes such decisions about problems.

STORY

Put the glass down - A Professor began his class by holding up a glass with some water in it. He held it up for all to see and asked the students, 'How much do you think this glass weighs?'

50gm!' .... '100gm!' .....'125gm' ......the students answered. 'I really don't know unless I weigh it,' The Professor said, 'But my question is: What would happen if I held it up like this for a few minutes?

'Nothing' the students said. 'Ok, what would happen if I held it up like this for an hour?' The Professor asked. 'Your arm would

begin to ache' said one of the students. 'You're right, now what would happen if I held it for a day?' 'Your arm could go numb; you might have severe muscle stress & paralysis & have to go to hospital for sure!' ventured another student and all the students laughed.

'Very good. But during all this, did the weight of the glass change?' Asked the Professor. 'No'. 'Then what caused the arm ache and the muscle stress?' The students were puzzled. 'Put the glass down' said one of the students. 'Exactly,' said the Professor.

Life problems are something like this. Hold it for a few minutes in your head and they seem okay. Think of them for a long time and they begin to ache. Hold it even longer and they begin to paralyse you. You will not be able to do anything.

It's important to think of the challenges (problems) in your life, but even more important to 'put them down' at the end of every day before you go to sleep. That way, you are not stressed, you wake up every day fresh and strong and can handle any issue, any challenge that comes your way.

So, readers remember - to 'put the glass down today'.

THE BEST IS YET TO BE

Problems are a part and parcel of life. For some problems are rare, but for many problems is a part of their life. When we have problems, we must never run away. We must be patient and hope for the best.

◆◆◆

29

FAILURE

Don't quit when you meet with failure. One of the most common causes of failure is the habit of quitting when one is overtaken by a temporary defeat. Every person is guilty of this mistake at one time or another. Failure is a stepping stone to success. Failure teaches us several lessons, the other word for failure is an attempt.

If failure is taken in the right sense, it can lead us to the top of the ladder. But at the same time if failure is not taken properly, it can be fatal for us. Failure has to be looked upon as a tool for our own growth in life. Failure teaches us lessons and if one does a proper introspection as to why failure has occurred, it will not surface again.

Failure is an integral part of life. It has existed since the birth of mankind. When you do something and it does not happen according to what you expect, you call that failure. Failure can come to anybody. Even the most successful person on this earth would have seen failures in life. Failures have taught people lessons, not to forget people who have ended their lives and have even gone mad because they have failed.

But the greatness of a person lies in failing many times and still having a flicker of hope that he will succeed one day. There are very few people to name even today. One such great example is Abhraham Lincoln – who tried and tried even after he failed several times in life. The other typical example is of Colonel Sanders, the founder of Kentucky Fried Chicken who went on trying his luck in spite of seeing failures.

There are different types of failures. They are:

1. Heart failure
2. Engine failure
3. Failure in studies
4. Love failure
5. Failure in business
6. Failure in relationship
7. Failure in life

Heart failure: This is a case where the heart refuses to function anymore. Once the heart ceases, man dies. If the kidney fails, we can replace it, even if any other vital organ of the body fails, we can rectify it and prolong it for some time, but when a man has a heart attack, he seldom survives. This again depends on the intensity of the attack.

Engine failure: Most engines are manufactured to withstand pressures. But in spite of all the research and hard efforts still the engine can fail. We cannot rule out the possibility of a failure at any given point of time. There can be a technical defect in an engine. An engine can fail and either stop functioning or there will be some defect in the engine.

Failure in studies: In spite of a person studying day and night, still he can fail as he will not be in a position to recall what he has stored in his brain. This leads to failure in studies. Most people fail in studies as they do things in the last minute. A whole hearted effort must be put in studies.

Love failure: All those who fall in love do not do it sincerely. When two people are in love it is nothing but attraction towards the opposite sex which is also called infatuation. There can be a failure in love due to difference of opinion or chemistry not matching.

Failure in business: Failure in business can occur for several reasons. One is, if a person has got a shop where there are many competitors, unless he sells in a unique way, he cannot succeed. The next thing is the person who does business must have the business acumen.

Failure in relationship: Many relationships fail as the partners fail to understand each other and look at things differently. The failures are mainly between spouses. At times the failures can be temporary, but it can also be permanent and lead to divorces. Most divorces are happening due to personal egos where partners do not get along with each other. Failures can happen even with our other relatives.

Failure in life: This is the ultimate. Today you will find a lot of failures in life. When you ask them only about 3% of them will say that they had failed due to their own folly. The others will say that they had failed because they were good but the people around them were bad. Many would also blame fate for their failure. The pity is many people take failures to their heart and land up as ultimate-failures in life.

Failure in life is the worst thing anybody can have; most often heart failure will eventually lead to death. A childhood friend of mine who is no more once commented at a funeral pointing at the graves, 'This is one of the most peaceful places for any human being buddy.' Three months later he died due to kidney failure.

According to me success has a thousand fathers, 'failure' is an orphan, nothing succeeds like success. Failure is a stepping stone to success. There cannot be success without going through failures. One has to go through failures if he has to succeed. Unfortunately many people, who see failures early in life, give up their quest and land up doing nothing. They blame fate. But a tough person will take failures as a challenge and confront and forge ahead in life.

I have seen the worst part of my life. I was in such a position that everything that I had, was gone. The worst part was people whom I trusted and helped when I was doing well seemed very hostile and they never wanted to help me. I was called unlucky. No one was willing to lend me money. They felt they would not get back the money even if they lent it. At this juncture I recall having given money to so many people even without asking them when they would return it.

There came a time when everything was lost. My pocket was empty. Friends had abandoned me. I began selling my things one by one. I felt I had come to the end of the road. But one thing was sure; I did have a flicker of hope in me that I would do well one day. I was a fighter from birth. I thought I should live and avenge all this humiliation. This was what I thought when I was in my dark days. That is just to take revenge on people who were responsible for my fall.

Suddenly there was a change in my life. Things began to show up. There was light at the end of the tunnel. I began doing well and I am in a position much better than what I was when I was doing well the first time in my life. I have learnt three things now.

That is:

1. Never to have friends
2. I had done some silly mistakes
3. Always be prepared for a fall.

Never to have friends: After all these bitter experiences I have decided to have limited friends, and I have kept them in their place and do not want to go out of my way to help them like the way I did in my earlier day. I believe 'once bitten, twice shy'.

I had done some silly mistakes: I had done some mistakes pretty well knowing that they were wrong. I am not doing what I did in those days, I have learnt several lessons.

Always be prepared for a fall: I have never saved anything in those days thinking days would always be sunny, but that was not the case. Today I have saved up money for the rainy days.

STORY

An oil well caught fire. The fire was too dangerous for the fire brigades of the company to go near.

Things were getting desperate. As a last resort, the local fire brigade was called.

The local fire brigade was notoriously inefficient. But to the surprise of everyone, it took the engine close to the fire and bravely put out the fire.

The grateful and appreciative oil company presented them with an enormous cheque for their bravery at a public reception.

After the ceremony, the head of the oil company asked them, 'How could you display such heroism where our own people failed?' They answered, 'Our engine was not fully under control because the brakes were faulty. The engine took us too close to the fire and there was no way but to fight it.'

Break failure proved to be a blessing in disguise to the fire brigades. Life, at times, may present unexpected turn of events that may bring fortune even when undeserved. Accept certain amount of mysticism in life.

Thomas Edison succeeded with the invention of the light bulb by eliminating all the things that didn't work more than a 1000 so called failures. Walt Disney created Disney Land from bankruptcy by successfully visiting over 400 banks before he found one that would lend him the money.

Neither one of these men focused on failure in fact their minds were not focused in the physical world. Both of them had a dream and their minds were focused in imagination where failure does not exist. It is a wonderful place where we have 100% control over the outcome, anything is possible and there are no limitations. If we stay focused we will always succeed. The so-called failure comes from interpretation of the images into physical life and the failures are simply a process of elimination taking away what does work to get to what does work.

Where failure is concerned success is pleasant and failure is bitter. The common idea that success spoils people by making them vain, egoistic and self-complacent is erroneous; on the contrary it makes them, for the most part, humble, tolerant and kind. Failure makes people bitter and cruel.

Edgar Guest says

'Learn the hard way through failures.
It is better to have tried in vain,
Sincerely striving for a goal,
Than to have lived the plain
An idle and a timid soul.
It is better to have fought and spent
Your courage, missing all applause,
Than to have lived in smug content
And never ventured for a cause.
For he who tries and fails may be
The founder of a better day;
Though never his the victory,
From him shall others learn the way.'

For some people failure is a lesson, for me failure is a stepping stone to success, but failure is also a disastrous end for many people who have taken failure deep into their hearts and have either ended their lives or have died due to internal combustion. If only people take failure as a lesson; something that is sent to us to test us life would be different.

THE BEST IS YET TO BE

Failure is a stepping stone to success. Many of us fail to understand this. We feel very bad when it comes to failure. We do not know if it is a test for us. When we fail we must wait. Hope for the best.

◆◆◆

30

MOMENTS IN LIFE

The moments that we have today, will be counted tomorrow. If we would have wasted moments yesterday, we will be called a waster. If we would have spent it wisely, our names will go down in history. Some moments are anxious for us, some time later, it becomes memories. Every moment is God's gift, make it memorable.

Moments of life are defined by the Creator, yet we can decide what to do with those moments. Take for example, God will send us 24 hours of time. How we spend that time will depend on what we will become in life. Some people will spend it wisely and learn things for the years to come. Many will waste it and pin the blame on God. The moments that we have must be utilised properly, yes we will have a combination of the following. They are:

1. Most Memorable
2. Very Pleasant
3. Pleasant
4. Good
5. Fair
6. Sad

7. Very Sad
8. Tragic
9. Sad for me, good for us
10. Good for us and sad for others
11. Tragic for all
12. Fruit salad Type.

Most Memorable: When I received the best boy of the year 1993 I felt I was on top of the world. That was the most memorable moment of my life.

Very Pleasant: Recently I was in Ooty for a vacation with my friend that was a very fine moment and a very pleasant one, I long to have many more like that.

Pleasant: Recently I got a huge Motivational Training order from an Engineering College in Coimbatore, it was pleasant news for me.

Good: A friend called me and said that my second car loan was sanctioned on the phone that was good news for me.

Fair: A trainer friend of mine who had left me came back after he got a battering from one of my competitors. I felt the news was good as well as bad, in general it was fair as I was not too excited about it.

Sad: I had an argument with my colleague for a silly reason. He could have avoided it, but he made a mountain out of a molehill without verifying facts. I was very sad, but of course everything is forgotten.

Very sad: A close friend of mine lost his leg in a freak accident. When I heard about it through a common friend I was very sad.

Tragic: Recently in Coimbatore, a youth who was riding a motorcycle and attending a cell phone was run over by a private bus. It was very tragic not only for his family, but for me too as I witnessed the accident.

Sad for me, good for others: An employee working with us left our organisation, as she was getting married. It was sad for me as she was an asset; it was good for her husband who was getting a good wife.

Good for us and sad for others: I got an order from a company to do business, it was good for us but it was sad for the company people who lost it to us.

Tragic for all: This is the time when we lost Indira and Rajiv Gandhi. It was a tragic moment for all of us except the terrorists who were behind the killings.

Fruit salad Type: This is a mixed type of moments where the good, the bad and the ugly can all be there and they can be there in kinds, variations and proportions.

Life can give us several moments. They can be memorable moments, happy moments, sad moments and a mix of both happy and sad moments. Much of what happens on how we take these moments. I know a lot of people who have had bad moments. They do not want to forget them; they live with them and then go to the grave with such bad moments in their memory.

I also know people who have had bad moments; they have taken things positively. One must forget those bad moments and begin a new life. Such people are happy. There are also people who have bad moments and still succeed as it does not pop up like the ones who think about only sad moments.

As a child my father snubbed, shouted at me, kicked me and made my life miserable. I would cry and would fear my father a lot. Do you expect me to remember all those bad days and brood over it, or for that matter do you expect me to take revenge on my father who is old, weak and dependant on me? No, I have just forgotten it. When I think of those moments, I just sit and laugh, sometimes I wish those times come again. At times, I sit with my father for a drink; we bring back old memories, I become very emotional when I think of those old days of life. Alas! It will not come back to us.

A year ago, I visited Hubli where I spent a part of my childhood from the first to the twelfth standard. I visited the place where we stayed. I walked through the streets where I spent my childhood, I also met people who were known to me and greeted them. I had lunch in one of my old neighbour's house. I sat in the playground where I played as a boy. I walked through the green fields where we all played and spent our holidays. I also made it a point to visit the cemetery where many of my neighbours were laid to rest. I prayed there and was silent. As I walked through the streets and looked at the houses, it brought back old memories. I was emotional and would have cried if I got an opportunity. I was so very thrilled that I had seen the place I spent as a child. I drove to the nearby colony where we had shops. I visited those shops and did some purchases. Some people recognised me others said they might have seen me. In the evening I had a small drink with some of my old childhood friends. Then, we had dinner and walked through the roads for some fresh air. I returned to Bangalore very sad, nevertheless that I had been to a place where I grew up. I cherish those memories even till today.

It is still a mystery as to why certain things happen. It is also not revealed as to why we are born to a particular couple. It is also very unclear as to why moments come, be it good or bad. This is something that is very tricky and difficult to answer, nevertheless confront at times.

Tit-Bits

Don't go for looks; they can deceive. Don't go for wealth; even that fades away. Go for someone who makes you smile, because it takes only a smile to make a dark day seem bright. Find the one that makes your heart smile.

Dream what you want to dream; go where you want to go; be what you want to be, because you have only one life and one chance to do all the things you want to do.

May you have enough happiness to make you sweet, enough trials to make you strong, enough sorrow to keep you human, and enough hope to make you happy.

The happiest of people don't necessarily have the best of everything; they just make the most of everything that comes along their way. The brightest future will always be based on a forgotten past; you can't go forward in life until you let go of your past failures and heartaches.

When you were born, you were crying and everyone around you was smiling. Live your life so at the end, you're the one who is smiling and everyone around you is crying.

Don't count the years--count the memories........... Life is not measured by the number of breaths we take, but by the moments that take our breath away!

Arty Pereira states, 'Enjoy every moment of your life. There is one striking common feature with all really successful people. They all look and feel young. That is because life to them is never boring – they enjoy every moment of life. You will also notice that their faces shine with expectancy, as if every next moment may provide a surprise packet in the form of a new idea, a new friend, a new hobby or a new enterprise. And they do not want to lose the chance when it comes. Many of the stupendous inventions of the world have resulted from a flash of inspiration which came to the inventor in a single moment. Of course, this was preceded by years of patient toil and trials.'

Who is this man?

There was a man who lost heavily in business at age of 20.
He was defeated in a legislative race.
At 22, failed again in business.
At 24, overcame the death of his wife.

At 26, a nervous breakdown.

At 27, lost a senatorial race.

At 34, lost his chance to be the Vice President.

At 47, but became the President of United States at 52.

He was Abraham Lincoln.

Can we call his life as a life of failures?

Failures are a stepping stone to success.

Akbar and Birbal were taking an evening walk. Suddenly Akbar said to Birbal, 'Tell me a sentence that if we read it in happy time we should become sad and if we read it in sad time we should become happy.'

Birbal replied, 'This time will pass away.'

Lastly I state that every moment that is given to us or that is ahead of us is in our own hands, it depends on how we make use of them. We can choose to waste them, we can also choose to use them judiciously or can leave it to itself to give us what it wants. Finally, I state that we have to make every moment of our life a masterpiece if we have to really succeed in life.

THE BEST IS YET TO BE

Moments in life are not defined anywhere. We still do not know why things occur and why we are in the position that we are; that is the good as well as the bad. All we are required to do is to wait for the best to happen. Hope for the best.

◆◆◆

31

KINDNESS PAYS

When you are kind you get paid in the same coin. Unfortunately people do not realise that being a little kind brings them great joy and happiness. They feel that if they are unkind, they are being strict. When we are kind to others God will be kind to us. We will have internal joy in our lives when we are kind.

Kindness itself is caring for the others, being gentle, friendly and also being generous. Not many people fall under this category. The very concept of kindness is a very complex question. We wonder why some people are kind. We also wonder why people are not kind. What joy does a person get when he is kind. What pleasure does a person derive when he is not kind. Why is that we have to be kind?

A person who is liked is the one who is kind. It is very clear that if a person is not kind, he will be disliked by all. You may have seen three kinds of people when it comes to kindness. They are:

1. The Kind people
2. The Unkind people
3. The Situational Kindness people.

The Kind people: Such people are liked by all. When a person is kind he is warm towards the others and he also understands the problems of the others. We have very few people in the world who are really kind. When I say 'really kind', I mean people who not only portray themselves as kind but they are also kind where action is concerned.

The Unkind people: We find every other person in the world today who is unkind. Such people take pride in being unkind. We do not know if they do it wantonly or if they are born with such a negative trait. All the more they are not liked by anyone. If a man is unkind even his wife and child will not like him.

The Situational Kindness people: There are people who juggle between being kind and not being kind at times. This may depend on their personal moods or it may differ from case to case. A man will surely be kind to his son, whereas he will not be kind to his neighbour's son. He does not know that in being a little kind, he is gaining the goodwill of the other people.

Kindness must come from the depths of our hearts, we don't need to go to a course to become kind. We have to learn and cultivate the habit of being kind in our lives. Many people who were unkind have changed and have become very kind and warm. There are also people who were kind have become unkind. Many factors could have driven them to change their behaviour.

All said and done, 'He is a happy person who is kind; and I have never heard of an unkind person having the internal satisfaction within himself.'

Kindness is a word that exists only in heaven. It is very rare to see persons who are kind. Kindness is something which is endowed to all humans, but unfortunately many people are very unkind and bring pain to others. One does not realise when he is kind, he is doing some good to the other person. When you are kind, you enjoy it so also the person you are kind to.

By being kind I mean the following. They are:

1. Helping people when they are in distress
2. Coming to someone's help when they are confronted with many problems
3. Pardoning someone who has done something bad to you
4. Sharing something with those who are in need
5. Helping someone financially
6. Giving someone something that you have and they don't have
7. Listening to someone sympathetically.

By being unkind, I mean the following. They are:

1. Hurting someone
2. Being cruel to people
3. Having something, refusing to give
4. Not willing to share
5. Seeing someone in poverty when you have riches
6. Insulting someone in public
7. Denying someone their rights.

You must also remember that kindness can be paid by kindness. What I mean is when a person is kind, nobody will be unkind to him. If he had a record of being kind to others, surely he will get only kindness. I once spoke to a person in fish shop who was removing the skin of the fish when it was yet alive, he told me that the fish had no soul and that it did not suffer any pain. I had to remind him that every living being with blood has pain and misery and we must not bring pain to them. Even while killing animals one must be kind to them.

When you are kind to others, it comes back to you. At the same time when you are rude or cruel, that too comes back to you but with a little extra force. Try being kind and see the difference. But do not be unkind or rude as it will not help you in any way.

Instead it will bring you enemies. People will begin to hate and may even avoid being with you.

There was an old man in Kerala, India, noted for his serenity. Nothing disturbed his calm, not even the gravest provocation. He had in fact become a curiosity for everybody in the village.

One day a few young pranksters decided that they would make him angry. They caught hold of a young ruffian, instructed him what to do, with a promise of Rs.100 if he got the old man to lose his cool.

The old man used to have a bath in a river every morning. The youngsters went and hid themselves among the scrub on the river bank. When the old man was returning from the river, the young ruffian went up to him and spat on his face. The old man just smiled, and went back to have another dip in the river. When he emerged from the river, the ruffian again spat on his face. Again the old man smiled and went back for another dip.

More than a hundred times the shocking spectacle was repeated. Ultimately, the young ruffian was defeated in his game. In genuine contrition he prostrated before the old man and asked his pardon. The youngsters, too, came out of their hiding and asked for the old man's pardon.

One youngster, who could not believe that a man could exhibit this amount of patience, asked the old man, 'Sir, how could you tolerate the atrocious action of that ruffian?

The old man replied calmly, 'After all he is a child.'

We love children. We forgive their mischief and continue to show them affection. Similarly if we are able to show love and affection to each and everybody in this world there would be no occasion for us to get angry or irritated. To reach this state of consciousness is not easy. It needs constant practice and diligence.

Poem

He ruled with an iron hand.
He never spared anybody.
He was merciless with everyone.
He never spares even his wife.
All those who came to him for justice got a whip
This went on and on.
Till one day, he had an attack of stroke.
The whole kingdom began praying.
They prayed not for his recovery.
But for his death and downfall.
He was overthrown by his nephew.
The nephew put him in a mental asylum
The king was breathing his last.
All those who were with him were his victims.
No one dared to even go near him.
He died in pain, agony, misery, all what he gave to others.
He got in turn with interest.

STORY

An unemployed graduate woke up one morning and checked his pocket. All he had left was $10. He decided to use it to buy food and then wait for death as he was too proud to go begging. He was frustrated as he could find any job, and nobody was ready to help him.

He bought food and as he sat down to eat, an old man and two little children came along and asked him to help them with food as they had not eaten for almost a week. He looked at them. They were so lean that he could see their bones coming out. Their eyes had gone into the socket. With the last bit of compassion he had, he gave them the food. The old man and children prayed that God would bless and prosper him and then gave him a very old coin. The young graduate said to them, 'You need the prayer more than I do.'

With no money, no job, no food, the young graduate went under the bridge to rest and wait for death. As he was about to sleep, he saw an old newspaper on the ground. He picked it up, and suddenly he saw an advertisement for people with old coins to come to a certain address.

He decided to go there with the old coin the old man gave him. On getting to the place, he gave the proprietor the coin. The proprietor screamed, brought out a big book and showed the young graduate a photograph. This same old coin was worth 3 million dollars. The young graduate was overjoyed as the proprietor gave him a bank draft for 3 million dollars within an hour. He collected the bank draft and went in search of the old man and little children.

By the time he got to the place where he left them eating, they had gone. He asked the owner of the canteen if he knew them. He said no but they left a note for you. He quickly opened the note thinking it would lead him to find them.

This is what the note said, 'You gave us your all and we have rewarded you back with the coin.' Signed God the Father, the Son and the Holy Ghost.

Take an opportunity to be kind to all, be it human or animals, whatever religion, caste, creed or gender they may be, be kind to them. You will see for yourself that you will be paid in kindness itself. If you are unkind, do not expect kindness. But if you are kind, even without expecting, you will get kindness.

THE BEST IS YET TO BE

When you are kind, people may be unkind, that must not stop you from doing good. Continue to do good. Be kind, if the rewards are not immediate, wait it will come but with a bigger wrapper than what you did. Hope for the best.

◆◆◆

32

MANAGE THE THREE-TIME, MONEY AND THOUGHTS

Management is an art which can be learned by anybody. It is not necessary that one goes to Indian Institute of Management to study management to manage things. A man who sells vegetables on the roadside is in a position to manage his time, money and also thought. It is a very simple process.

I have learnt one thing in my life. This is my experience; it is also the experience of three people who I know very closely, and especially the ones who are highly successful in life like me. We have to manage three things effectively in life. There are also other things which we have to manage effectively, but I am emphasizing on these things for now. They are:

1. Time
2. Money and
3. Thoughts.

I feel if we can manage these things first, we can manage the rest as well.

Time: Time is essential for all of us in life. We have been gifted twenty four hours by our creator. Some of us know its value and make use of it. Many do not know its value and realise it very late. Some do not realise it even when they are dying. I still do not understand how people can say they do not have enough time. These are the people who wake up early in the morning and spend an hour thinking in bed whether to wake up or not, they spend another one hour in sipping coffee and reading the newspaper.

Make a careful use of your fragments of time. It is wonderful how much can be got through by these means. A great deal of study, or writing, or other work, can be done by a resolute will in odd quarters of hours, and very often we can get no more. Nothing is more commonly said that if you want something done, you will have a much better chance of getting it done by a busy man than by an idle one, and this is simply because the former has learnt the secret of economising his time.

They spend another hour in having their breakfast and by the time they decide what to do, it is noon and time to have lunch and when food goes in, it's time to sleep and then wake up and have tea and by the time tea time is over, it is time to sit in front of the idiot box and now dinner time approaches. How can he or she do anything when they are so busy?

Orison Swett Marden says, 'Beware of how you spend time, for all your future lives in it. Time is money. We should not be stingy or mean with it, but we should not throw away an hour any more than we would throw away a dollar bill. Waste of time means waste of energy, waste of vitality and waste of character is dissipation. It means the waste of opportunities which will never come back. Beware how you kill time, for all your future lives in it.'

Time Poem

Take time to live
It is the secret of success

Take time to think
It is the source of power

Take time to play
It is the secret of youth

Take time to read
It is the fountain of wisdom

Take time to be friendly
It is the road to happiness

Take time to laugh
It helps to lift loads

Take time to dream
It can show you the way

Take time to love
It needs to be nurtured

Take time to give
It is too short a day to be selfish.

Money: Money as I told you in the earlier chapter is essential for all of us. We must earn a particular amount and spend a little less. Many people earn ten rupees and spend twelve rupees. These two rupees extra come from something we call 'credit'. These days we have an 'evil' called credit cards. Several people fall a prey to this evil. They spend money on the credit card even without thinking how they will repay it. They then get into trouble.

Banks offering credit card will lure you with all benefits and attractive schemes just to trap you and when you cannot pay them, they will put pressure on you and come to your door-step, even if this is not possible they will send goons to threaten and harass you. Hence I advise you not to fall into this trap set by banks that offer credit cards. You have to learn to manage money and spend it wisely or else you will be in a soup.

How to double your income in three years? Any man can double his income, in three years. All he has to do is to observe a couple of rules. First do only the things you know. Secondly don't do the things that you do not know, especially something you cannot do.

The irony of accumulating vast wealth while so many are languishing in misery is a grave transgression of God's law, with the consequence that the greedy, avaricious man is never at ease in his mind; he is in fact the most unhappy creature.

It is better to keep money away as it can be a very bad company for us. When you don't have any money, no one will even look at you. But when you have money, everyone will want to be with you, even a crow which is flying above your house will stop over to see what is happening. When you do not have money you can leave your door open and go out, but when you have money you have to appoint a couple of security guards to keep you protected.

One must have money enough for his sustenance and must not have more of it, the moment you have more of it, with that will come the tax authorities and several people to be your friend. Hence it is desirable that you have enough money so that you can have a peaceful life. After all when you go to your final resting place what you carry is nothing but just the goodwill of the people.

In a remote village in Karnataka lived a money-lender called 'Ayyu' who was a miser and a very ruthless man. He usurped several people's property. When he died people spat on his body, no one would come forward to carry his dead body. His son had to take the body in a cart and bury his father on his own. Does anyone need such a fate?

Here's a beautiful poem on money

Money can buy pleasure
But it cannot buy happiness
Money can buy cosmetics
But it cannot buy beauty
It can buy medicines
But not good health
It can buy sporting equipment
But not a good physique
It can buy good things
But it cannot buy goodness
It can buy a good coffin
But it cannot buy a good death.

THOUGHT

'Your life is what your thoughts are.' A person who can control his thoughts will be a master of his mind. We get a lot of thoughts, the good, the bad and the ugly. For some it is a combination of good only where the bad and the ugly are less. For many the bad dominate where ugly is second and good ones are last. For several people the first thing is ugly thoughts, next comes bad thoughts. Only at times do good thoughts come.

Your thoughts, not your body, are your real self. Mental attitude is a far more powerful factor in your daily, hourly existence than perhaps you may imagine. Your thought is as real as blood, muscle and sinew. It goes from you to others, acts on them, moves and influences them. This is your real power; and as you learn how to control and project it, you will come to play successful as a great player.

One can have good thoughts only if he has clean habits. You must love people, the world and nature in general, only then will you get good thoughts. It is very easy for a person to fall a prey to bad and ugly thoughts, whereas it is quite difficult for a person to get into good thinking. Good thinking is like climbing up the hill which is not easy, bad and ugly thinking is like coming down the hill. It comes very easily. Any person who can control his thoughts, can control his life and that of the others depending on him.

Ralph Waldo Trine says that thought is the great builder in human life. The same grain taken as food by two persons will be converted into the body of a criminal in one case, and into the body of a saint in the other, each after its kind; and its kind is determined by the inner life of each.

And what again determines the inner life of each? The thoughts and emotions that are habitually entertained, and that inevitably, sooner or later, manifest themselves in outer material form. Thought is the great builder in human life; it is the determining factor. Continually think evil thoughts, and your life will show forth in evil and your body in weakness and repulsiveness. Think thoughts of hatred, and you will hate and will be hated. Think thoughts of good and you will flourish and will be liked by others.

Thought is a mighty creative force. Before man can progress, he must realise that thought is a mighty creative force. Each thought, therefore, activated by strong feelings of fear or desire is a creative act which seeks to externalize itself in the form of some experience, constructive or destructive.

STORY

This story illustrates how a person can manage situations when he is confronted with one. The court jester kept the king in good humour with his quips, and entertained the royal household.

On one occasion the king was displeased with a retort of the jester and condemned him to death. But after a while the king realised the rashness of his decree. It was however supposed to be legally impossible for the king to change any sentence he set on a subject. So he asked the jester: 'In consideration of your faithful services, I will permit you to select the manner in which you prefer to die.' The jester instantly answered:

'I select to die of old age.'

With presence of mind and intelligence one can manage any situation in life.

THE BEST IS YET TO BE

All of us are not good managers. We fail at times. When we fail we must not lose hope as there is still a lot to go. We must wait for the right opportunity. The true manager in us at times will take time to manifest. Hope for the best.

◆◆◆

33

LEISURE-PLEASURE

One must have leisure with dignity. A poor life that is, full of care, we have no time to stand and stare. Man is the only living being that is endowed with the gift of leisure, make the best out of it, forget animals and birds that have no work and relax, their lives are always in danger from predators and human beings.

There is a great thinker who has said, 'Leisure is best when there is hard work before and after that.' That is, one has to work hard for a period with enough money to spare for the next season and then take off on a leisure trip. After his enjoyment he has to again go back to work as he cannot afford to continue with his leisure trip unless he has a fortune and he wants to spend it.

I have seen people seeking leisure depending on their likes and dislikes. My own example is, I will never seek leisure unless and until I am sure that I have no official work to do. Even when I take time for leisure my mind is always working on my official business.

Same is the case with pleasure, I do not say that man does not need any pleasures. As far as I know man is the only living being that enjoys pleasures of life at the cost of the other living beings which we control. The only other living beings that enjoy pleasures to some extent are the pets (dogs and cats) we have in our houses. They too have pleasures like good food, walks and some entertainment like us human beings.

My father would love leisure and would go for it at the drop of a hat. Whenever he found time he would take off for some trips to holy places or places of interest. He would also plan picnics and outings. Whereas his own brother was just interested in amassing wealth and using that money for some investment. Whenever his children wanted some type of entertainment he would send them to a local park or to some cheap form of entertainment. While one brother wanted to enjoy life, the other was saving money for his twilight days.

I had the opportunity to speak to both when they were quite old. I would fear talking to either my father or my uncle as we had great respect for them, it is only now when they were a little old that we got to move closer to them. My uncle is no more whereas my dad is 85 years of age.

Here's what my father and uncle had to say:

My Father: My father always felt that leisure was good for us. He asked, 'What is the use of all the money we earn and store; we have to enjoy it when we are alive. We do not carry it when we die. Hence a reasonable amount of leisure is essential.'

My late Uncle: He always had an insecure feeling right from his childhood days. He said, 'We have to keep money for the rainy day, I do not believe in spending money for leisure as I feel it is a waste. This is something you don't get back. If we use the same money to buy a gram of gold, the price will go up and that is how I look at it.'

I find three categories of people when it comes to leisure. The three categories of people are:

1. Leisure seekers

2. Work seekers
3. Fortune-leisure seekers.

Leisure seekers: These are the people who always seek leisure even without working. At times they go to such an extent that they borrow money. They not only spend money for themselves but they also spend money for their friends and relatives.

Work seekers: Such people do not want any leisure, they just want to work and save money. Under this group you have two categories; one is the group that is on a hand-to-mouth basis, who say they cannot afford leisure. The other group can very well afford leisure but they say it is not meant for them and that is meant only for those who have money and opulence.

Fortune-leisure seekers: This category of people sit on a fortune left behind by their ancestors and only enjoy life. There is also another category which adds up to the fortune left behind by their ancestors.

Leisure and pleasure are interlinked. When it comes to leisure it can have both the good as well as the bad side.

The good side is:

1. Holidaying with spouses and family
2. Relaxation and Meditation
3. Decent Partying
4. Trekking
5. Picnic
6. Vacation to a relative or a near or dear ones place
7. Pilgrimage

Holidaying with spouses and family: Holidaying especially after some hard work is essential, time for family is also essential as it is also a part and parcel of life. After all what does man work for? His food, shelter and some entertainment.

Relaxation and Meditation: Relaxtion is essential for all human beings. When one relaxes his mind and body are still and the cells recover from the wear and tear. Meditation is also essential as God speaks to man through meditation after one prays to Him.

Decent Partying: Man is a social animal and has a lot of needs, wants and desires and hence there is nothing wrong in partying so far as limits are kept and decency maintained. Parties are given for two purposes, that is when there is an occasion and second when there is a birthday or an anniversary or to thank and pray for somebody for some favour.

Trekking: Trekking is also required as it not only tones up your muscles, but also gives joy and some adventure. It has to be done when one is free and not at the cost of one's work or business. Trekking must also be done in safe and known places.

Picnic: Picnics are also essential especially after some toil. Picnics are arranged for people to enjoy in groups. This is an opportunity for persons to relax, have fun and socialise apart from going to see places of interest.

Vacation to a relative or a near or dear one's place: Going for a vacation with family and friends is a form of pleasure that is also a leisure, but what we do there is most important, we have to make it memorable and enjoyable rather than make it soulful.

Pilgrimage: A pilgrimage is meant for noble purposes whereby devotees are required to pray, worship, do penance and keep away from any form of addictions. This is the best time to recharge our batteries and recover from any mental tensions that we would have had.

The bad side is:

1. Drinking
2. Smoking
3. Gambling

4. Drugs
5. Prostitution
6. Indecent partying
7. Pleasure trips without family.

One must take up the first category and avoid the second one. One must also be careful about one thing when it comes to leisure. Nothing must be done in excess. There must be a limit for everything. We also have to plan our finances and go on leisure trips only if we have the money, we should not borrow money. Leisure can also be planned well in advance and it can be either at our own place or outside.

Also remember certain things. As human beings we are entitled to leisure under certain conditions, that is we have the money and the time. Secondly do not do it just because others are doing it. The next important thing is you have to choose the good ones and not the bad ones. Once again I state 'leisure is best when there is hard work before and after it'.

We have lots of time to focus on our thoughts. Most people do not have the luxury of taking time to relax and think. Okay, we did not ask for these 'time outs'. They are demanded by the needs of our bodies. Nevertheless, we have control over how we use this extra time. Instead of dwelling on what our bodies are not doing, give your fantasy full liberty. Turn these rest periods around to be indulgent time. In our mental playground, we can practise dance steps we used to know (for there will be some times we can dance). We can use the time to think through problems we face and how we want to spend time when we are feeling ready, or we can analyse a movie we recently saw, say prayers, or mentally write a letter to a friend.

STORY

There were two friends Amal and Raj. Amal was fond of pleasure whereas Raj was not fond of leisure but he would have fun at the cost of Amal.

Amal was a fun loving person and spent most of his time in partying, going on vacations and enjoying life. He began spending away all his money.

On the other side Raj was saving money. He began buying gold and invested in small pieces of land. Amal would make fun of him for buying land in a remote place that was not inhabited by man. The same land has fetched Raj a huge sum. Amal sat with his face hanging in shame.

The time had come for both to retire, while Raj had lands, gold and investments running into several crore that were invested as thousands. Amal did not have anything. He had only fond memories of parties, good week-ends and record of having eaten all types of meat and the best of liquor. He didn't own a house and was at the mercy of his children who would ill-treat him.

Raj on the other side had become a landlord; he had gold and money at his disposal. He commanded respect not only in his family but with the others too.

THOUGHT

> Laurie Lee says, '*Learn to give up pleasures regularly. One of the major pleasures in life is appetite and one of our major duties should be to preserve it. I think we should arrange to give up pleasures regularly, our food, our friends, our lovers in order to preserve their intensity and the moment of coming back to them.*'

Any right thinking person will select the good leisure as his pastime and convert them to pleasures. If we sit back and think and see the money that we have spent for good things compared to the bad ones that we have invested upon, we will surely gain where the good ones are concerned and lose where the bad ones are concerned.

Any person spending time in reading is likely to increase his knowledge in leaps and bounds. It is believed that 'a person who eats too much will become a swine' and 'a person who reads a lot becomes learned'.

At the same time if one were to sit back and see how much money he has spent on drinking, there will be no gains except some momentary pleasure for him. Even in gambling a person may or may not earn money, all the more even if he earns money it is someone else's hard earned money that he has snatched through unfair means.

THE BEST IS YET TO BE

Leisure and pleasure are not given to all, neither do all of us who seek it get it. If we get it we are lucky. We have to use it judiciously, if we don't we have to wait and work for it. Hope for the best.

◆◆◆

34

OUR POTENTIAL

'What lies before us and what lies behind us are small matters compared to what lies within us.' Most often we are more interested in what the man in front of our house is doing. We envy him. We compalin and gossip about people who do well. If we look back, we have a lot of potential within us and seldom use it.

All of us human beings are born with a great amount of potential. Many of us use it, some don't use it and many people are not aware of it. All those who know about it try to make the best use of it. Those who try using it give up half way as they fail, they think that their potential is limited or they assume that it is just a hoax and a false belief.

There are three types of people as far as potential is concerned. They are:

1. People who use their potential to the fullest
2. People who do not use their potential in spite of being aware of it
3. People who do not know about it and live life ordinarily and go to the grave without using it.

People who use their potential to the fullest: There are very few who belong to this category. One such person whom I have heard is Thomas Alva Edison and Albert Einstein who made great use of their potential. The rest have made the graves rich by taking their potential to the graves unused.

People who do not use their potential in spite of being aware of it: I know quite a lot of people who sleep over their potential in spite of knowing it. I recently met a Professor who is highly intelligent and has taken voluntary retirement from his teaching. I met him, he said that he wanted to rest in life. I felt he was wasting his potential that he had within himself.

People who do not know about it and live life ordinarily and go to the grave without using it: A majority of the people can achieve success but they neither have the confidence nor know how to use it. They go to the grave with all the potential. I was in Ooty and met a milkman who knew the Presidents and Prime Ministers of India right from Dr. Rajendra Prasad and Jawahar Lal Nehru to the current President Pratibha Patil and Prime Minister Manmohan Singh. When I asked him to take up teaching at some village, he laughed and said, 'With my education, if I teach, this country will go to dogs.'

Where potential is concerned I also need to touch upon another topic and that is about the three types of people who exist on this earth. They are:

1. Thinkers
2. Doers
3. Thinkers and Doers.

There are also the other categories of people who neither think, nor do anything. These people are a waste to society and live life just to make a misery of someone else's life.

Thinkers: These people are the ones who use the maximum of their brain power and think a lot before doing anything. They analyse the situation and order other people to do a particular thing. These people have conviction in their abilities and do the thinking. There are a very small percentage of such people.

Doers: These are the type of people who can think, but they feel that their thinking is not as good as the thinkers and hence they are happy doing what the thinkers ask them to do. In fact these types of people dominate the thinkers and doers.

Thinkers and Doers: These are the type of people who have a twin talent; they can think as well as do it. They think when they have to, and do when they have to do it. They do the thinking and wait to pass it on to the doers, but if the doers don't turn up, they do it themselves. Such type of people are very rare to see.

I spoke to nearly 50 (students and adults) people and got a fair idea about the percentage. They are:
Thinkers - 13%
Doers - 77%
Thinkers and Doers - 10%.

It is believed that the brain has got small nerve cells called neurons. Each cell can do several functions. A human has got several trillions of such cells. Many people are not aware of the existence of such cells, whereas the people who also know about them do not believe in it. The main difference between a millionaire and a beggar is primarily in their thinking. A case study was conducted sometime ago on the body of a millionaire and a beggar. The persons who did the autopsy found that there was not much difference in the organs and the other cells in the body. Both were the same. That shows that the man who landed up as a millionaire used his potential more than the beggar whose needs were small.

We made a small study among the students for whom we conducted a workshop on soft skills. These are the names that we got from them.

People who used their potential in those days were:

1. Thomas Alva Edison
2. Henry Ford
3. Alexander Graham Bell
4. Albert Einstein
5. Orville and Wilbur Wright
6. James Watt
7. George Bernard Shaw

People who are using their potential for the upliftment of the world today are:

1. Bill Gates
2. Sabeer Bhatia
3. Richard Branson
4. A P J Abdul Kalam
5. Narayana Murthy
6. Lakshmi Mittal
7. Azim Premji

The tragedy with many people is that they think they do not have potential in them. Most of them get stuck to such convictions that they do not even want to try out something, in spite of knowing that they too can make it. We had a boy working with us in our household when we were children.

Every time he saw us kids doing something good, he would appreciate us and say 'very good, well done'.

On one occasion my grandmother asked him, 'You always praise the kids, why don't you do something similar?'

He smiled and said, 'Where is their upbringing and where is mine, I can't do ten per cent of what they do.'

This was embedded in his mind. He still continues to do badly in life and is dependent on us for his survival.

Hence I must state that when man is created, we come with the same potential, but what we do with it, will depend on what we actually become in life. Some use it and make the others work for them, while the others do not use it and land up working for the ones who use their potential. Everyone of us must believe that we possess that potential and must put it to proper use or else we will sit and envy people who do well in life.

STORY

Generally fisherman venture out into the sea at night and bring their catch early in the morning. One such fisherman named Mani went out in the sea at six in the evening. He returned from the sea early in the morning at around five and waited for dawn to sell off his catch and go home. He had a moderate catch with him which was not too less and not too much too.

He sat by the water throwing small pebbles into the water. He was restless not knowing what to do. He then paced up and down looking at the waters and partially at the sky. He walked into the water and looked in all directions.

After a while he sat down, lit up a beedi and began smoking. That too did not satisfy him. He kept walking up and down and now he began walking farther always keeping an eye on his catch, which was in the seawater. The reason why these fishermen keep their catch in seawater is to keep the fish alive. If it is out of water, it will die and then begin to decay. No one would like to buy old fish especially on the shore where the buyers have a lot of options.

Mani was pacing up and down and very casually he kicked a bag of pebbles. He lethargically picked it up and shook it and found a jingling noise. He unfastened the bag and felt its content. He realised it was a bag of small pebbles may be numbering a hundred or so. He then began throwing them one by one in the water.

This is what we do when we have pebbles in our hand and are seated before a stream, lake or sea. I used to do this when I was a child near our farmhouse, which had a lake. I would spend a large amount of time in throwing pebbles in water, which gave me some pleasure as a child.

Now it was Mani's turn to empty the bag of pebbles into the sea. He had thrown all those ninety-seven of them into the water and was curious to know as to who had taken the trouble of putting these pebbles into a bag and to know what were its contents. All that he assumed was that it was pebbles.

It was now turning a little bright and things were seen around. Mani took those three pebbles left and looked at them closely. They were precious stones. Alas!

He yelled out. 'What did I do?' He was shocked and angry with himself; he kicked the ground and realised his folly. But things very too late.

Message

We are all like Mani in some way or the other. We throw things unconsciously and waste our precious time. If ever we were to know how precious things are, we would not be throwing them away. It is only after a loss or realisation that we know how important things are. Some of the things we throw away unconsciously like the fisherman are: time, energy, talent, words, knowledge, opportunities, etc. In other words we throw away our lives and repent later.

THE BEST IS YET TO BE

Some of us realise our potential very early, many realise that they have a potential very late and hence they just sit and assume that they cannot become achievers. One has to wait and try to explore his potential. Hope for the best.

◆◆◆

35

MONEY IS NOT EVERYTHING

The man who thinks that money is everything is a sentimental fool. You may have tons of money but if there is nothing to buy, then what use is that money that you have. There could be a case where you have tons of money and no one is willing to part with anything for exchange of money. Then what is the use of money? Hence I state money is not everything.

If God appears to man and asks him what is that one thing that he would like to have among the three choices that he offers – health, peace and money, I am sure 99% of the people will ask for money. It is only those people who have money and are fed up will ask for health and peace and that too after asking God for more money and later on realising that money is not everything in life. People are so obsessed with money.

Here's a dialogue with God. He called on five people and here's what they said to God. They are:

God – well son I have three wishes for you (health, peace and money) which of the three you would like to have?

Person 1: I would like to have tons of money at my doorstep.

Person 2: I would like to have all the riches of the world that are available.

Person 3: I would like to have all the gold in the world.

Person 4: Please give me a little money and also my health as I have almost lost it.

Person 5: Lord! Please give me just health, as I have no use for the money you gave me.

In ancient days there was a barter system where goods were exchanged for goods. There was fairness and people were not greedy. As always a group of people who wanted to have more with them came out with the concept of small copper coins which then became brass coins after which metal coins were made. It was during this time that toll, tax and cess were also being levied by kings and hence the concept of money came in and has become popular and since then money plays an important role in man's life.

Money has existed from ancient days. Money is essential for us human beings to buy what we want, in other words to make a living for ourselves. But if you look at what has happened to money today, one will really feel sad. In those days people used to work hard for money and earn it. Today we have people who do nothing and earn lots of money. The actual people who work hard do not get enough money. There are certain groups of people who do not work hard for money. They are:

1. Politicians
2. Real Estate Agents
3. Rowdy Elements

Politicians: Politics has become a game of rascals and a last resort for a scoundrel. Today majority of the people in politics are either criminal or criminal-minded. If one is not criminal-minded he will not shine in politics. In fact the qualification for getting into politics is one must either be a rowdy or a union leader. There are very few good leaders today. Today if people want to make easy money they have to do these types of business. They are:

a] Enter Politics
b] Start an educational Institution
c] Start a Temple or a Church.
d] Real Estate Agents
e] Rowdy Elements

Enter Politics: This is a very easy way to earn money as a politician who threatens people or uses his governmental powers and makes money.

Start an Educational Institution: This is another way to make easy money. Gone are the days when missionaries would start schools and colleges to serve the people through education. They were doing a minimum profit just for survival. Today it is just the other way around.

Start a Temple or a Church: This is the latest way of doing business. Any lazy person who is a little street smart will come up with an idea and start a temple stating that he saw the vision of God. Same is the case with bogus Pastors who say they saw God in their dream and will start a small Church just with an idea of fooling the innocent people to make easy money.

Real Estate Agents: Today every lazy person has become a real estate agent and wants to make fast money without any toil. They dress up like netas and go around showing people some property and make money from both the sides. They do not pay tax and live in opulence. They connive with politicians and rowdy elements to do their business.

Rowdy Elements: Today this has become business. The rowdies operate right under the nose of the cops who are hand-in-glove with them. A notorious rowdy is arrested and a criminal lawyer comes to his rescue. The local politicians hire such people to win elections. Rowdies make huge money with very less toil.

One must work hard for his money or else it will not remain with him. Even if it remains it is a curse. Many people hoard money and do not bring it out. All this is a result of insecurity. Money is such a powerful tool today that people kill one another and also get their near and dear ones murdered just for money.

I have read incidents such as:

1. A businessman got his brother murdered as he felt by murdering his brother he would get a bigger share.
2. A son murdered his father just to get all the money which was with his father.
3. A man insured his wife for a huge sum. He then took his wife by car to a hillock, pushed his wife and driver and claimed they had an affair and committed suicide. He got the money from the insurance company.
4. A daughter got her father killed as he refused to part with some money that she wanted to do her higher studies.
5. A woman connived with her paramour and got her husband killed to get possession of his wealth.
6. A woman got her son killed as she was unable to access the money that was left behind by her late husband.
7. A man got his father, mother and brother-in-law murdered as he wanted to inherit the wealth of his wife.

Wealth leads to dharma as well as happiness in life, if it is acquired with discrimination in the right way and without evil. The chief advantage of wealth is the security it gives. A man of wealth may venture on any action, in that splendid security with which a man looks on an elephant-fight from top of a hill. He enjoys all the pleasures of adventure and of triumph without anxiety as to possible reverses.

I know a friend who has a lot of money which he earned by way of buying and selling properties. He has so much wealth that he can hardly sleep at night. He has taken to drinking and smoking heavily. His wife has left him. He has a plethora of diseases and spends a lot of time in medication. When I met him he said that he was far better off when he had no money. He claimed he was happy with no money, but now he is in misery with money minus peace and good health.

Most of those people who have money in excess are the ones who have exploited and earned it by unfair means. If a person runs a business, he has to be unfair to save a lot of money or he is in the wrong business. No person who is honest will have excess money with him.

If all the people in India pay taxes properly, we would have had a good society where there is no poverty, we will have good roads and a better functioning government. Today the government cannot do much as nearly sixty per cent of the money is hidden by people who earn it the wrong way. If all that hidden money comes out, we will not have problems in the economy.

Cricket players and film stars are paid in crores. If we look at their contribution towards nation-building, they literally do nothing. Whereas the jawans who guard our frontiers get a pittance. The farmer who slogs it out in the sun and rain to grow crops for us gets a pittance. There is a lot of imbalance. Unless we boycott these celebrities and give reasonably to the ones who work hard, we will continue to have problems.

My conclusion is as follows. A certain amount of bank balance is required for our rainy days; earn money in the right manner. Be fair and do not exploit anyone. Ensure that you have enough money where you will be in a position to answer the doorbell.

Where you will walk free on the roads. Where no Income Tax man will chase you and no one will curse you for having made money in the wrong way.

A great thinker says:

Take a cigar daily – you will die ten years early.

Drink daily alcohol – you will die five years early.

Love money – you will die daily.

STORY

This is a very famous story of a miser in France, who never even married for the fear that he might have to share his money with the family. He had a secret cellar in his house, to keep all his treasure. He would go down there regularly every night, admire all his treasure, and come out. He would save every single penny to add to his treasure.

Once, he wasn't seen around for many days and soon the days turned into months and the word spread of his mysterious disappearance all over the town. Since there was no one to claim his property and the house, it was legally taken over by the Government and then sold off to someone.

After a long time, the new owner found the cellar while building an extension in the house and to their surprise, the miser's stinking dead body around the glittering gold and jewels. In his mouth was a candle piece. This would mean that he might have tried to appease his hunger by even trying to eat the candle.

One cannot be considered as wealthy just by collecting and accumulating large amounts of money. Greed only leads to misery. True wealth lies in what you are and not in what you have.

Message

Too much of money can lead to problems, if only the miser had to make use of the money, but then again a miser is a miser.

THE BEST IS YET TO BE

We see a lot of people with tons of money, whereas there are several people who have nothing at all. They are even uncertain about the next meal. The man who wants money will get it, but he has to wait for it, unless he is born in a wealthy family. Hope for the best.

◆◆◆

36

UNBURDEN YOURSELF

Most of us in life carry tons of loads on our backs, they are not physical but not visible to the human eye. I am referring to burdens that we carry. These burdens are intangible. They are so heavy and occupy a large space in the brain that there is hardly any room for us to think creatively. In our workshop, we have something called 'Catharsis' where we help participants unburden themselves.

Many people with all the wealth in the world keep complaining about something or the other. They always have some excuse to think about. I know a lady who has everything, but she keeps grumbling all day long. One day I asked her what was her problem. She began by stating that everything was a problem. She was carrying a lot of mental load in her head. She found fault with almost everything around her. She would curse everything including water, the vegetables, the rice which she brought and the meat that was purchased. She also targeted her daughter, her husband, her grandchildren and all the people around her. The only person whom she did not complain about was her pet dog whom she liked.

Some people are born like that. When we see such people we have to do three things, one is to advise them to some extent, second we have to learn from them 'what not to do'. The last thing is we have to find out why they behave in such a manner. All people who are problematic have some history behind them.

The reason why I state we must not have a burden is when a mule is overburdened it staggers to move along and struggles as it is meant to carry a particular weight and if it exceeds the weight, it becomes difficult for the animal to carry weight. This is something to do with the body. Our minds are also governed by the same facts where if it is full especially with garbage, it cannot function properly. That is why, we have to either desilt our minds like the way water tanks are done or we have to unburden ourselves by way of getting counselled or phasing out the negatives we have within us.

Unburdening is not possible for all persons. Some can do it, others can do it partially and some may not be in a position to do it at all. The types of minds that people usually have are as follows. They are:

1. Firm Mind
2. Steady Mind
3. Vacillating Mind
4. Loose Mind
5. Useless Mind

Firm Mind: There are very few people with this mindset and they can successfully unburden themselves, that is if they possess any type of problems.

Steady Mind: This type of people can also go ahead with the process but with a little bit of guidance from counsellors.

Vacillating Mind: This type of people cannot unburden themselves as they have a mind that will not be firm in its command. Usually people with this mind have to live with negatives in their minds (if they have any).

Loose Mind: A person with this mindset will not be in a position to either control his mind and also not in a position to unburden himself. He can do it only partially and that too with a strong guide to help him out.

Useless Mind: People with this mindset cannot do any rectification. Even if they try to do it, it will not work. Only a percentage of it will work for them.

Man carries several burdens in his head. If we write it down the list will be huge. Here are some common burdens that man carries. They are:

1. Worry about not having money
2. Worry about having too much money
3. Family problems
4. Health problems
5. Relationship
6. Uncertainty
7. Fear of failure

Several people have genuine problems, but many people worry for petty things and unnecessarily burden themselves. For some carrying burdens are a way of life, for many it comes as a routine, for some it comes as a shock. People who are possessive tend to have many such burdens in life. There is a process that can happen in one's life where carrying burdens can be phased out over a period of time.

Only people who belong to the first two categories can do the unburdening process successfully. They have to go in for counselling and get the rating of their minds and then go about this action.

It is not necessary that people with the categories will all have negatives in their minds. It depends on the person and their individual mindset.

A young girl who attended the JADE workshop had a very sorry tale to tell. She was raped by her uncle and grand-father when she was about fifteen-years-old. She was at the mercy of these two people as she had lost her father. Her mother was out of town when this incident took place. The mother could not do anything as these two culprits were funding her education and bearing their expenses from the day the girl's father expired. She had no other go but to leave the house after this incident.

The girl is now grown up and she got a job in Bangalore and began running the family. She happened to attend my workshop where she argued that the culprits must not be spared. I told her that she was the loser and not they. She wanted to avenge her rape. But I was against it. I just helped her unburden herself through a catharsis therapy which worked for her. Today, she is relieved and has forgotten the past and is now confident that she will marry and conceive. I requested her not to reveal this incident to her would-be husband as it would cause complications.

Our minds are very sensitive. The human mind once damaged cannot be retrieved or even repaired. Hence we have to be extra cautious about the mind. Our mind has got a certain capacity. It has the ability to hold the good, the bad and the ugly. While some people hold only good things in mind, many people hold unwanted things in it and keep recalling them and suffering. They like to tell people about their problems and they expect the ones listening to them to sympathise with them.

Man is the only animal who talks to himself. All day long you carry on an inner conversation with yourself about your problems and opportunities, the people and events around you, the things happening in your life. As you will see, your inner communication is an important part of you in fact, it is you, and it does indeed, 'behove' you to become aware of it and use it to your benefit.

One can unburden the mind of unwanted things through certain ways. Before that one needs to know what is required and what is not required. Only after this segregation is done, can a person go for formatting. This is similar to what is done to the hard disks of our computers. A back-up has to be taken and then the formatting process is done. But the process of what is done in a computer is different from that of the minds. In a computer all the data can be removed, but that is not possible in the mind. It is a huge process that requires quite a lot of efforts, time and dedication. Only after all these things are done can we really go ahead with the process.

When the mind has to take in new things, it needs space to store the new data that is fed inside and if there is no space, the old and negative ones must be phased out to facilitate the new ones to enter and be stored.

The process of unburdening can be done only if a person is firm on his or her decision. This is not an easy process and it has to be done systematically. We must first agree to forgive others. The negatives that are in our mind are the ones that cause such irritants. We have to remove such irritants and then go ahead with the reconstruction work.

After one has resolved to unburden himself, he has to do the following without which it may not work. They are:

1. Resolution
2. Frame of Mind
3. Counselling

Resolution: A person must take a resolution to get him do the job. This consent must come from within himself, no one must force him to do so, if they do they will be imposing it on him.

Frame of Mind: The person going for it, must have a positive frame of mind without which he cannot go for it, even if he goes for it without having a clear mind, things will not work.

Counselling: The reason why a person has to go for counselling is because a person's mind will have knots and issues that have to be phased out. Only if hurdles are removed can there be a clear road to proceed.

STORY

Once upon a time a big monk and a little monk were travelling together. They came to the bank of a river and found the bridge was damaged. They had to wade across the river.

There was a pretty lady who was stuck at the damaged bridge and couldn't cross the river. The big monk offered to carry the pretty lady across the river on his back. The lady accepted.

The little monk was shocked by the move of the big monk. 'How can big brother carry a lady when we are supposed to avoid all intimacy with females?' thought the little monk. But he kept quiet.

The big monk carried the lady across the river and the small monk followed unhappily. When they crossed the river, the big monk let the lady down and they parted ways with her.

All along the way for several miles, the little monk was very unhappy with the act of the big monk. He was making up all kinds of accusations about the big monk in his head. This got him madder and madder. But he still kept quiet. And the big monk had no inclination to explain his situation.

Finally, at a rest point many hours later, the little monk could not stand it any further; he burst out angrily at the big monk. 'How can you claim yourself a devout monk, when you seize the first opportunity to touch a female, especially when she is very pretty? All your teachings to me make you a big hypocrite.'

The big monk looked surprised and said, 'I had put down the pretty lady at the river bank many hours ago, how come you are still carrying her along?'

THE BEST IS YET TO BE

Many of us have invisible burdens that we carry against our kith and kin. Sometimes it is so heavy that we cannot move ahead in life. We have to remove them if we have to forge ahead. It depends on our will-power to do so. Hope for the best.

◆◆◆

37

LOVE ONE ANOTHER

Love one another and make a heaven on this earth. If we love one another, we will not have hatred. No wars, no greed, no borders, and no military force and there will be peace all over. We will enjoy God's creation to the fullest and the best. There is more joy in loving one another than in hating a person.

When I say love one another, it also means that we must not hate any person for whatsoever reason it may be. Hating people has become a trend today. The world is no more what it was in ancient times when people were more united, understanding and humble. Today we find just the opposite of what prevailed in ancient days. These days we can see a father murdering his son just because a son marries a girl from outside his community. We also see brother fighting and even killing one another for money. We also see business partners who ditch each other just for the sake of money.

If we have to do all this we must love one another without considering caste, creed and religion. For this we need to have a ego-free mind, a certain amount of humility and concern for fellow human beings in the world. If these things are there, then one can surely love one another.

The reason why I have included this chapter in this book on self-improvement is, that it has got a direct connection with our development. When we talk about best, there is actually no best without 'love' and when I say love it is not just a generic word that we hear of today. In my opinion there are three types of love. They are:

1. Love of some objects
2. Love of parents, siblings and relatives
3. Love of a spouse

Love of some objects: We love cars, bikes; we also love certain food; we love doing something, may be reading. We love music, we also love watching movies. That is about love related objects that you are fond of. The one thing I must tell you is learn to love everything and never hate anything. Alternatively, if you love something go with it; if you don't like anything don't show it off as someone may love what you do not like.

Love of parents, siblings and relatives: This is a very sacred love where you show affection to your loved ones in a true sense without any physical relationship. Even if you kiss, it will be a holy kiss like a father kissing his daughter or a mother kissing her son.

Love of a spouse: This could be a love that penetrates deep inside ending in physical relationship. This love is only between the opposite sexes to put it in a true sense. I do not want to comment on what the British singer Elton John does with his partner. Here the love is something that is intimate and lead to sex for producing children. There are also people who love someone apart from their spouses which is called 'extramarital affair'.

Now let me come back to the heading 'love one another'. The reason why I have selected this topic is after seeing what is happening in the world today.

The world is in chaos; it is no more the good old world with decent people inhabiting it. The mentality of people is changing drastically. People are going from bad to worse.

Here's what is happening in the world.

Some examples are as follows:

1. Countries are waging war against each other.
2. One brother is pulling the other in court for property disputes.
3. Spouses are playing with their life partners engaging in extramarital affairs.
4. Parents are setting a wrong example of staying in separate bedrooms.
5. One is plotting against his own brother to overtake him in business.
6. One sister is setting her parents against her sibling for gain.
7. One neighbour is against the other and is engaging against them by wrongful acts.

In an island, all the feelings lived. One day there was a storm, the island was about to drown, every feeling was scared but love made a boat to escape, every feeling got onto the boat, but one feeling was missing. Love got down to see who it was. It was ego. Love tried and tried but ego was'nt moving and water was rising. Everyone asked love to leave him and come to the boat, but love was determined not to move without ego. At last love died with ego.

Jesus himself has told mankind in one of his parables 'love one another as I have loved you'. Every human being must and should love his fellow human beings. If we look at the world today, the rate of people loving the others is as less as three per cent. No one wants to love the others as he feels it is a burden for him.

I still remember my days in the late nineties when I was down and out; I was doing very badly in business. Everything that I attempted was a failure. I had an angel in my older brother who supported me with conviction. There could have been two things in his mind, one is he has to look after his younger sibling as it was his duty. On the other hand he may have had the hope that someday I will rise and do well in life. That is what siblings are meant for? He did feel that I was a gone-case at times and decided to stop supporting me, but he would only tell it out externally. He never meant it; he saw to it that I did well in life. He has never given me an opportunity to repay him as he is far ahead of me in life. One of the reasons for his success could be, because he helped me make it up in life.

STORY

In order to renovate the house, someone in Japan tore open the wall. Japanese houses normally have a hollow space between the wooden walls.

When tearing down the walls, a man found that there was a lizard stuck there because a nail from outside hammered into one of its feet. He sees this, feels pity and at the same time curious, as when he checked the nail, it was nailed ten years ago when the house was first built.

What happened?

The lizard has survived in such position for 10 years. In a dark wall partition for 10 years without moving, it is impossible and mind boggling.

Then he wondered, how this lizard survived for 10 years without moving a single step - since its one foot was nailed!

So he stopped his work and observed the lizard, what had it been doing and what had it been eating? Later, don't know from where appears another lizard, with food in its mouth... AHHH! He was stunned and touched deeply.

For the lizard that was stuck by nail, another lizard has been feeding it for the past 10 years.

Such a love, such a beautiful love. Such love happened even on this tiny creature. What can love do? It can do wonders. Love can do miracles.

Imagine it has been doing it for a tiresome ten years, without giving up hope on its partner.

Imagine what a small creature can do when a creature blessed with the brilliant mind can't.

As the technology advances, our access to information becomes faster and faster. But the distance between human beings, is it getting closer as well?

What we learn from this story is not to abandon our loved ones.

Humour Time

Four men were bragging about how smart their cats were:

The first man was an Engineer, the second man was an Accountant, the third man was a Chemist and the fourth man was a Government Employee. To show off, the Engineer called his cat, 'T-square, do your stuff.' T-square pranced over to the desk, took out some paper and pen and promptly drew a circle, a square, and a triangle. Everyone agreed that it was pretty smart.

But the Accountant said his cat could do better. He called his cat and said, 'Spreadsheet, do your stuff.'

Spreadsheet went out to the kitchen and returned with a dozen cookies. He divided them into 4 equal piles of 3 cookies. Everyone agreed that it was good.

But the Chemist said his cat could do better. He called his cat and said 'Measure, do your stuff.'

Measure got up, walked to the fridge, took out a quart of milk, got a 10 ounce glass from the cupboard and poured exactly 8 ounces without spilling a drop into the glass. Everyone agreed that it was pretty good.

Then the three men turned to the Government Employee and said, 'What can your cat do?' The Government Employee called his cat and said. 'Coffee Break.....do your stuff.' Coffee Break jumped to his feet........ ...ate the cookies..... .... drank the milk........ sat on the paper....... screwed the other three cats........ claimed he injured his back while doing so..........filed a grievance report for unsafe working conditions.. put in for workers compensation. .... and went home for the rest of the day on sick leave.

Guy in the Glass

Dale Wimbrow says, 'When you get what you want in your struggle for self, And the world makes you king for a day, Then go to the mirror and look at yourself, And see what that guy has to say.'

For it isn't your father, or mother, or wife, whose judgement upon you must pass. The fellow whose verdict counts most in your life is the guy staring back from the glass. He's the fellow to please, never mind all the rest.

For he's with you from clean up to the end, and you've passed your most dangerous, difficult test if the guy in the glass is your friend. You may be like Jack Horner and 'chisel' a plum, and think you're a wonderful guy, but the man in the glass says you're only a bum if you can't look him straight in the eye.

You can fool the whole world down the pathway of years, and get pats on the back as you pass, but your final reward will be heartaches and tears if you've cheated the guy in the glass.

THE BEST IS YET TO BE

Many of us are starved of love. We have tremendous wealth but no love. Even those people, who love us, do it just for our money. In such a case we have to win people's hearts rather than purchase it. If we don't get love we have to wait. Hope for the best.

◆◆◆

38

WHAT TO DO, WHAT NOT TO DO

What you do, and you feel is right may not be the same in the eyes of the others, whereas the same principle can apply for you where a person is doing something which he feels is right and wrong according to you. The only solution is that you do something which is acceptable to all. Learn to do what is right and not what is not right.

One must know what to do and what not to do. There are several things we have to do. At times we do it on our own, most often we wait for commands from others. There are many things which we should not do. We, at times take command from others and at times we ourselves learn to desist from it. A person who is mature in mind will know clearly what to do and what not to do. It is better that a person writes down the things he has to do and also the thing that he must not do. As I said earlier if a person is sensible enough he will know what to do and what not to do, another thing is one must also know when to do things. We must be doing the right things at the right time and also be doing the right things in the right place.

In every walk of life we can learn two things from people. That is what to do and what not to do. It depends on the individual that we are observing. When you see a person, all that he does may not impress you. You may like certain things and may not like certain things in him. At times you may not like anything in a person. There are also cases where you will like everything in a person.

I have written this chapter for a simple reason and that is if all of us had to follow this, the world would have been a better place to reside in. I have, for convenience given examples of trainers as it is my field. This is what I had seen and experienced. But the idea and concept remains the same.

I had the privilege of working with one of the greatest authors and trainers in India. I am referring to Dr. Francis Xavier who is my guide and mentor. He had his own ways whereas I had my own ways.

Whereas I was in favour of getting up very late as I would work till late in the night, he was an early bird and would go to bed early and wake up early. This did not affect our working in any way, but to a large extent I saw his ways of working. During the course of my stay with him I learnt two things. They are:

1. What to do and
2. What not to do

What to do: This is something that you can learn from many people whom you come across. This is mainly the good that you see in people. But you must be careful about one thing. If a great person does something which you feel is good, that does not mean it will be good for you as well, it can also be bad in the eyes of the other people. Hence you have to analyse what you see and then decide whether to imitate or not.

What not to do: These are pre-dominantly bad habits in people. It could be speaking ill or even general habits that are not good. You must be careful about one thing and that is what is bad in your view may be right in someone else's case. What I mean by bad things is to be adaptable and not put others in trouble.

Let me cite some examples. They are:

1. You may want to smoke but you will be putting others into inconvenience.
2. You may want to eat non-vegetarian food, but the others with you may not want it, according to you, you are right, but the others feel you are not right.
3. You may want to sleep extra time, whereas your spouse or anyone with you will see you as lazy person.
4. If you are in a common room and want to study till late night, you switch on the lights, the other person may be put to inconvenience.
5. When you are in a group, you must know group behaviour techniques / rules and ethics.
6. You may want to play music, but the other person may want silence, you have to adjust yourself.
7. You may want to do something that others will not like, but yet you want to go ahead with it, you have to consider others when you do something.

When you see people observe two things in them. One is see the good that they do and imitate it. At the same time look at the bad that they do and vouch that you will not do it. Today I head a very successful training organisation that is not only reputed, but also in great demand. I adopted a unique strategy to build up JADE Training Resources Private. Limited. Many things constitute my success, one such thing is the way in which I observed and am still observing trainers.

I study the wrongs and thereby decide what not to do. In the initial stages when I worked for other Trainers and their Organisations I observed their mistakes and registered in my mind and told myself; 'If I start my own company, I will not do this.' That has gone a long way in my success.

I had the opportunity to work with a few trainers and observed every action of theirs. I also had the privilege of attending the training programmes of great people. When their programme was going on what I did was something different from what many people do. Generally people will learn what to do and try to imitate them, but I began thinking differently and visualised as to 'what I would do if I were to be in their place'. This gave me a lot of insights into training and also building my personality.

Here's what I had seen in people which I term as mistakes. They must not be done by a trainer. They are:

1. Losing our temper in front of students
2. Bad mouthing / Slander
3. Being obsessed with money
4. Working with a focus to earn money
5. Using vices
6. Bad habits
7. Unethical standards.

These are some of the things that I observed. There are many other things that I had seen which I will not do. I have only tried to bring in an example of this training field just to throw light on how you could get two things from people, that is what to do and what not to do. Even if you are with a genius, learn what not to do.

As we are touching upon this topic, we must not forget one thing and that is while we observe people, let us not look at a person just to find fault with him. We also have to look at the other side of a person. You may come across a case where all the people will talk good about a person and you may not like something. Nothing should stop you from airing your views about it.

There are also chances where all the people may not like something about a person whereas you have something good to speak about it, go ahead and give your views.

There are some people in the world. If they like a person, they will like whatever the person says and does, they will also expect you to endorse it. At the same time if they don't like a person and even if he is speaking sense or doing a good job, they will put him down. They will expect you to endorse even these views. You have to do a balancing act here to safeguard your own interest, depending on who the person is whether you are obligated to him or he is obligated to you. However it is better to keep away from such people in your own interest.

Once a donkey lay dead. All the people were poking fun and commenting. They were saying look how its stinks, another said how bad it looks and see how the stomach is bloated. There was a voice which was heard by all 'Look even in its death how sparkling its teeth is.' People were shocked and wanted to know who this person was. It was Jesus Christ.

STORY

This is a story on the evils of alcohol. A teetotaller was speaking on the evils of alcohol. Unlike other speakers, he was questioning the audiences much to their joy. You see when people are asked to sit and listen to a lecture, they get bored. For a change if the speaker adopts a method of asking questions the audiences will like it. He began by asking.

'Who has the big home in this town?' he said. 'Whose wife has expensive saris and precious jewellery? I will tell you who: the wine shop owner. And you my friends, you pay for this luxurious life.'

At the end of the lecture one young couple came to thank him for the most inspiring lecture he gave.

'I am pleased that you are going to give up drinking,' the teetotaller said.

The couple responded..........

The Query: What did the couple say to the teetotaller?

'Not exactly!' the couple said. 'We have been thinking of entering into business and your wonderful lecture gave us the motivation to start a wine shop.'

Everyone has his own way of interpreting something according to his own convenience. Depending upon the type of reaction that we have for a variety of stimuli, our character and conduct are developed.

THOUGHT

If you think you are beaten you are;
If you think you dare not, you don't;
If you want to win but think you can't;
It's almost a cinch you won't.
If you think you'll lose you're lost;
For out of the world we find
Success begins with a fellow's will;
It's all in a state of mind.
Life's battles don't always go
To the stronger and faster man,
But sooner or later the man who wins
Is the man who thinks he can.

THE BEST IS YET TO BE

We fail to understand what to do and what not to do. When we do something, it is right according to us but wrong from the other person's angle. Hence we have to wait for our opportunity to get attention. Hope for the best.

◆◆◆

39

KNOW YOUR DESTINATION

When we buy a gadget, we get a book that tells us what to do and what not to do. We call that book a 'user manual'. The manufacturer guides as to how the gadget must be operated. But when man is born he does not come with a 'user guide'. As we grow up in age and move with people and watch things happening we tend to learn many things in life.

If a driver of some bus were to just start the bus and keep driving without knowing its destination, two things are likely to happen. One is he may reach a place that he should'nt be in and secondly he may land up at the wrong place where he may run short of fuel and even food. Hence he must know where to take the bus.

Same is the case with a ship that has set sail without a destination. The captain of the ship should know where to steer his ship, lest he take it to an abandoned and lonely island which is infested with wild animals and savages.

In every walk of our life, we have to be prepared to know our destination. We must know where we are heading. If we do not know where we are going, then we will land up somewhere. At times that somewhere can bring us fortunes, but that is very rare and we only gamble over it. We have to know where we are going and we must also prepare to go there fully equipped.

If we are going to a place that is cold, we have to take our warm clothes. If we are heading towards a place where the fuel is uncertain we have to fuel the car. If we are going to place that is infested with thieves, we have to arm ourselves.

Based on the place we have to be fully prepared before we go to the place. We must never take chances or we must never do any guess work and land up in trouble.

Knowing our destination can happen through three ways. One is we just walk onto a road and that road becomes our future. The other one is we are forced into a road by our elders and that road becomes our future and the third one is we try all the possible roads and finally land up on one road and that makes a future for us.

Here are the names of seven people whose destiny has taken a drastic change. They are:

1. Chakroborthy
2. Sonia Gandhi
3. Abdul Kalam
4. Rajanikanth
5. Jaffer Sharief
6. Abraham Lincoln
7. Saint Augustine

Their details are as follows:

Chakroborthy: A Chemical Engineer in India has become a top CEO of an Express Service Company.

Sonia Gandhi: A lady who was a baker's daughter has become a prominent politician in India.

Abdul Kalam: A scientist who helped in making missiles became the President of India.

Rajanikanth: A bus conductor has become a super star in South Indian Films.

Jaffer Sharief: A politician's car driver became a Union Cabinet Minister.

Abraham Lincoln: The son of a cobbler became President of the United States of America.

Saint Augustine: A convicted criminal became a Saint and is venerated by millions of people all over the world today.

What do we understand from the above examples? A person doing engineering will have only his field in mind, but he lands up doing something else in life. That does not mean to say one has to deviate from his original stand.

Take my own example, the way in which I was brought up and did my studies and fought for my rights in life was almost in line with that of being a lawyer. But I have become a successful Trainer, an Author and a Personal Coach which is totally different from the legal profession.

Many of us turn out failures in life because we do not know where we are going. I asked one of my friends where he was going in life? He said, 'I am just going, let's see where I land up.'

I asked another friend the same question, 'Where do you think you are going?' He said, 'I am going like anyone else, I may land up somewhere; I will decide whether to stay there or to move further.'

I asked another person the same question; he said, 'I know very well where I am going,' he also told me the speed at which he was going, his stop-overs and the things that he was carrying when going out. I asked him what were those things.

Case Study

Here's a case that took place between a fisherman and a well educated person. We can see what the uneducated and educated meant and how they justified their roles in life and business.

A boat docked in a tiny village where a tourist complimented the local fishermen on the quality of their fish and asked how long it took him to catch fish.

Not very long they answered in unison. Why don't you stay out longer and catch more? The fisherman explained that the small catches were sufficient to meet their needs and those of their families.

But what do you do with the rest of your time? We sleep late, fish a little, play with our children, and take siestas with our wives. In the evenings, we go into the village to see our friends, have a few drinks, play the guitar, and sing a few songs. We have a full life.

The tourist interrupted and said, 'I have an MBA and I can help you. You should start by fishing longer every day. You can then sell the extra fish you catch. With the extra revenue, you can buy a bigger boat'. And after that?

With the extra money the larger boat will bring, you can buy a second one and a third one and so on until you have an entire fleet of trawlers. Instead of selling your fish to middle men you can then negotiate directly with the processing plants and maybe even open your own plant.

You can then leave this village and move to a big city and settle there. From there you can direct your huge enterprise. How long will that take? Perhaps twenty five years replied the tourist. And after that? Afterwards? Well my friend, that's when it gets really interesting, and answered the tourist laughing.

When your business gets really big, you can start buying and selling stocks and make millions. Millions? Really, and after that? Asked the fishermen. After that you will be able to retire, live in a tiny village near the coast, sleep late, play with your children, catch a few fish, take a siesta with your wife and spend your evenings drinking and enjoying your friends.

'That's what I am doing now', replied the fisherman.

A person walks up to a ticket office at a railway station and asks the clerk 'give me one ticket please'. The man at the counter is perplexed and asks 'where?' The man is blank. Such is the case with many people in the world today.

One has to specify exactly where it is you want to go, otherwise no ticket. No further action can take place. The lack of being able to give a destination has a further effect. How will you know if you have arrived at your destination if you did not know where it was in the first place? You have to know where you are going; you have to know what your objective is.

If you jump into a car, start the engine, start to accelerate, but don't make good use of the steering wheel, your journey will arrive at a destination very quickly! That destination though, will very likely not be your choice and could potentially leave your life in ruins. So take hold of the wheel and guide yourself forward to the destination of your choosing.

I was once delivering a lecture on focus and our future. I told my participants about our destination. Immediately a group of girls went to see an astrologer and wanted to know their destination. The astrologer gave them some standard predictions.

When they came back to me and told me about it I said that knowing our destination is something we ought to know where we will be some years down the line for which focus is important. I clearly know where I will be five to ten years down the line. My predictions may not be accurate but I will be somewhere near what I predict. I am confident of achieving things in a way I want them to be.

1. I would have established myself as an international author.
2. I would have established my company in all principal cities and towns in India.
3. I would have at least ten million in my bank account.
4. I would have appeared in major television channels.
5. I would have set up my dream project (National Centre for Learning).
6. I would have earned more credentials as an author, trainer and a social worker.

7. I will be getting ready to enter the Indian Parliament.

The road to success will not have the word S U C C E S S written on it. It will have an empty board which one has to take. The road to success will be taken only by those who dare to walk the road. Those who take the road with a firm conviction will land up successful persons. As such one has to know where he is heading or else he will take a deviation and land up at the wrong place.

STORY

A man ventured out into the world to a certain place. He travelled from place to place and reached a spot where two roads took an intersection. He wondered which road to take. He looked around here and there and then saw a man seated on the roadside.

He walked up to him and asked him, 'Good man where do these two roads lead to.'

The man looked at this stranger and asked him, 'Where are you from?'

The man replied, 'It is not important where I am from, but please tell me where these two roads lead to?'

The man asked the stranger, 'Where do you want to go'?

The stranger was silent for a while and replied, 'I do not know myself.'

The man then looks surprised and told the stranger, 'Then take any road, what difference will that make.'

THE BEST IS YET TO BE

We walk towards our destination. For many that is the right one. For several that is the wrong one. For some it is confusing whether it is right or wrong. If you are in the right place, good. If not wait. You will land up in the right place. Hope for the best.

◆◆◆

40

STOP REWINDING

Most people are obsessed with rewinding the past. They like to talk about how they were hurt, humiliated, insulted and had tough days. They tell it out of joy and fill their minds with this scrap. Such people even take revenge and do not talk to people who may have hurt them. By doing this they are only bringing doom to their lives.

I am writing this chapter especially for people who keep talking about two things. One is the way in which they were insulted in life and the other one is their own story which most often is a bore. If a story is told to a person once, it is good for the ears, but if it is repeated too often, it will become a bore. I had a boss in one of the company's I worked. He would call me into his cabin and keep telling me all his old stories when he was in the Indian Airforce. He had the habit of repeating it so often that we were all fed up. We had no other option but to listen to him as he was our boss.

As I write about this chapter I have two people in mind. Incidentally both of them were doing very bad in life in the initial stages of their life. Later on luck began shining on them and both became prosperous. One person began to enjoy life by forgetting his past. He was concentrating on his new business, his new found opulence and also the good days that he enjoyed. He hardly spoke about the past and that too when someone reminded him about it.

The second person who is no more also began doing well in life and had all the wealth at his disposal. He began something called the 'rewinding policy of negative things in life', which is never healthy for any man in this world. He spent all his time and energy in complaining about the past. He began searching for the people who ill-treated him. While he wanted to seek revenge, the other person wanted to actually thank the ones who had battered him as he felt they were responsible for what he was today.

I reside in Bangalore and we have a very famous lake called the Ulsoor Tank. For many years this tank was filled with dirty water flowing from all the gutters around this area. There came a time when there was only 20% water and the rest was mud. The Congress Government in the state came out with a very good plan that is to desilt the lake. They awarded a contract and emptied the water from the lake. Then the mud in the lake which was very dirty was also emptied into several trucks and sent to the outskirts of the city. The mud was sold as manure. After a few rains the lake got filled up and now we find clean water.

You may be wondering as to why I am writing about desilting here. I have a very close friend who keeps complaining every now and then. I took him to this lake and told him this story of desilting. Then I compared the lake with our minds. We tend to have a lot of unwanted things in our mind, especially bad events that may have occurred when we were young. If we want to feed our mind with good things there must be place for that. If the place is filled with unwanted things then there will be no room for good things to be stored.

This friend whom I am referring to visits me whenever I am in town. He spends about two to three hours chatting with me.

Nearly 80% of his conversation goes in complaining about his siblings, relatives and friends. The irritating part is he is in the habit of narrating the same tale over and again. I had to remind him that I already know the story. I also have to remind him to keep the story short as he is in the habit of making it very long. Another thing is when he calls me he does not even bother to ask me if I am free to talk to him, he does not care even if I am eating, he will go with his stories till I decide to hang up. He brings out new stories and that too created on his own, his whole life is a series of assumptions.

Here are some of his assumptions:

1. They speak ill of me
2. They have insulted me
3. They are jealous of me
4. They hate me for a very long time
5. They will do anything to see me humbled
6. They don't want me to do well in life
7. They are my sworn enemies and they are doing several things against me.

Some people are fond of rewinding the old things that would have occurred several years ago. There is nothing wrong if you rewind the good things that had taken place in your life. You can tell it to the other person with a lot of joy. But it is not advisable to rewind and go on telling what had happened several years ago. When a negative trait is embedded in the mind, it is difficult for the mind to discharge positive energy.

You may have heard of this word rewinding in an audio or a video player where you can view what is already passed out. This is good where good memories are concerned, but not where the bad phases of life is concerned. If I like a song or if I like a sequence in a movie and if I am watching it on a DVD player, I like to rewind and view it again. This is done when it comes to funny scenes.

Rewinding old and bad things is also a cause for many ills in life. People tend to exhaust their positive energies for unwanted things such as rewinding negative things and turn out losers. When people rewind negative things, here's what can happen to them. They are:

1. Early Death
2. Diseases
3. Lack of Focus

Early Death: One of the secrets of longevity is a pure and clear mind. When man carries all negative things in his mind, he tends to cut short his life like partial suicide. Hence a person who rewinds negative things in life dies early.

Diseases: Diseases originate from contaminated water, polluted air and adulterated food. That is what we have grown up with. But diseases originate from the mind and that too a burdened mind that is filled with unwanted things.

Lack of Focus: When man has a plethora of complaints, he has only one thing and that is whom to talk to about his grouses and how to take revenge on people who have insulted or troubled him. His energies go towards these things and hence he loses focus in life.

One of the factors that pull down a person in life is ever complaining and hence is seldom successful. If you look at all the people who have succeeded and those who have failed, you will find people who complain are the losers and the ones who phase out things are successful in life. I used to carry negatives earlier but after I gained a little fame and money, I thought it would be wise to spend my energies in forgetting bad things and looking ahead in life rather than thinking about the bad events and going to the grave with those negative factors which are of no use to anyone.

It is time you stop rewinding things of the past, forget it, phase it out and take it as a challenge and do not carry it forward, like a child of God forgive those people who did bad to you. You will lose nothing, but will only gain. If you are clear in mind, you will not have anything to regret later on in life.

Recently, I met an old friend of mine who used to be my neighbour in the early nineties. We bumped into each other at a super market. He introduced me to his wife. He spoke to me for a while and took my contact number. He came to my flat and discussed certain things about his wife. She was mentally disturbed and was on treatment. While all medicines had failed he depended on psychiatrists who fleeced him on some pretext. He took her to every counsellor possible.

After hearing him I asked him to bring his wife to me. I spoke to her, she sounded normal, and she was upset because they were childless. I immediately understood her requirements. She was with me for about two hours. All the time she complained about one person or the other. She never spared anyone including her husband. I then met her husband and told him only one thing and that is she must have someone to listen to her. He immediately started working on it and found a woman who stayed with them and conversed with her all day long. Now this lady is in good health and does not need a doctor or a psychiatrist. She is undergoing a good therapy and that is someone to listen to her woes that are healing her mind.

THOUGHT

If you look at a positive thinker try to be like him
If you look at someone thinking negative, avoid being like them
If you see people complaining, listen to them, but try not to do it
If you have complaints, keep it to yourself
If it is serious tell it to them, but forget it then and there and clear your mind
Do not carry it forward.

STORY

The one thing man must learn is to appreciate what he has and not what he does not have. Women in some parts of Mexico are fortunate. In these parts hot springs and cold springs cascade side by side. The women often boil their clothes in the hot springs and rinse them in the cold springs.

A tourist, who had watched this natural phenomenon fascinated, remarked to his Mexican friend, 'I guess the women think of old Mother Nature as pretty generous.' To which his friend replied.

'No, Sir. There is much grumbling because Mother Nature supplies no soap.'

We never appreciate what we have but only complain of what we lack.

Edward Murphy in his poem says – you are building your mental home all the time. Your thought and imagery represent your blueprint. Hour by hour, moment by moment, you can build radiant health, success, and happiness by the thoughts you think, the ideas which you harbour, the beliefs that you accept, and the scenes that you rehearse in the hidden studio of your mind. This stately mansion upon the construction of which you are perpetually engaged is your personality, your identity in this plane, your whole life story on this earth.

THE BEST IS YET TO BE

For some people complaining has become a part and parcel of their lives. When we ask them to stop complaining they say they are happy doing it. They also feel their problems will be solved if they complain. Let us hope that such people transform. Hope for the Best

♦♦♦

POPULAR SCIENCE

Fully Illustrated in Colour

9496 A • Rs. 120/-

2215 S • ₹ 165/- Available in Hindi also.

Contains 10 Projects

2214 S • ₹ 165/- Available in Hindi also.

FREE Tutorial CD

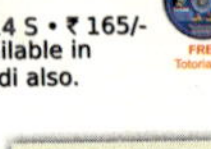

8716 T • ₹ 160/-

8733 D • ₹ 195/-

9660 K • ₹ 295/-

8702 B• ₹ 150/-

6678 D • ₹ 195/-

6679 A • ₹ 150/-

QUIZ BOOKS

8965 D • ₹ 150/-

7726 K • ₹ 120/-

7727 L • ₹ 120/-

7723 F • ₹ 100/-

9412 C • ₹ 150/-

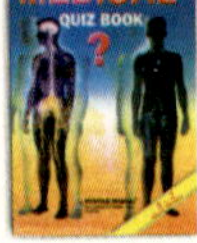

7753 G • ₹ 120/-

7725 B • ₹ 100/-

7722 E • ₹ 120/-

NEW RELEASES

8767 C • Rs. 120/-

0019 R • Rs. 160/-

8762 P • Rs. 140/-

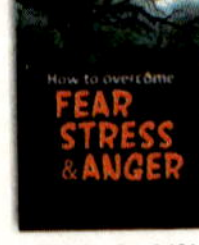

8764 T • Rs. 160/-

- Over 900 Illustrations
- Over 800 Pages
- 890 Articles
- Four Volumes

FREE Buy all 4 Vols. & get 5th Volume free with an Audio-Video DVD worth ₹ 135/-

All in Colour

Set Code: 4514 S

Set 4 Vols.: ₹ 780/-
Each Vol.: ₹ 195/-

Available in Hindi & English both

This Library is must for every student *of a* School *or* a College

Also equally useful for everyone else

Price: ₹ 600/-
Contains 4 books of ₹ 150/- each

4 Books of the Library

₹ 150/- Page 266 (with CD) English Conversation
₹ 150/- Page 310 Grammar & Punctuation
₹ 150/- Page 316 How to use English
₹ 150/- Page 344 English Vocabulary

Miscellaneous

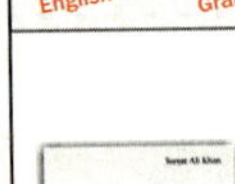

9497 B • ₹ 120/-

9783 H • ₹ 150/-

9680 B • ₹ 295/-

9686 H • ₹ 120/-

SELF-IMPROVEMENT

New

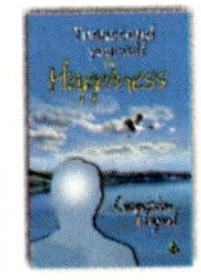

9698 R • ₹ 195/- 9498 C • ₹ 180/- 9490 H • ₹ 175/- 9464 R • ₹ 80/- 9096 B • ₹ 150/- 5614 E • ₹ 150/- 4008 J • ₹ 150/- 9026 D • ₹ 120/- 9786 M • ₹ 195/-

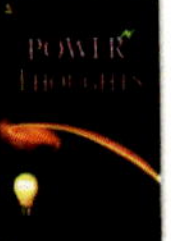

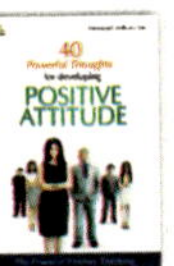

9491 J • ₹ 100/- 8885 D • ₹ 150/- 9081 D • ₹ 150/- 9091 B • ₹ 120/- 9060 B • ₹ 195/- 9684 F • ₹ 195/- 8928 D • ₹ 80/- 9449 A • ₹ 195/- 9788 R • ₹ 195/

MANAGEMENT/JOB/CARRIER/BUSINESS & PROFESSION

All Time Bestsellers

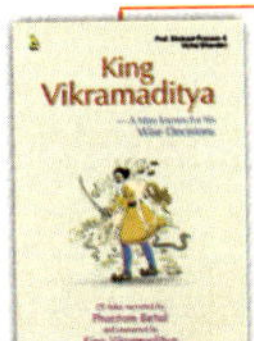

9461 K • ₹ 150/- 5338 A • ₹ 135/- (with CD) 8979 A • ₹ 135/- 9406 B • ₹ 150/- 9672 G • ₹ 150/- 9682 D • ₹ 120/- 8729 T • ₹ 120/-

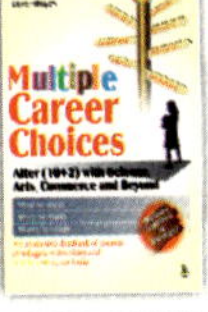

9697 P • ₹ 195/- 9313 D • ₹ 150/- 5623 B • ₹ 250/- 9439 L • ₹ 150/- 5441 D • ₹ 195/- 8883 D • ₹ 150/- 8735 F • ₹ 150/-

4018 D • ₹ 150/- 9079 B • ₹ 195/- 4005 E • ₹ 195/- 5643 B • ₹ 120/- 9431 C • ₹ 175/- 8990 C • ₹ 96/- 9763 P • Rs. 195/-

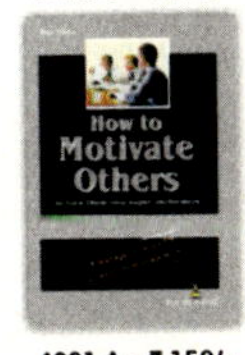

5618 D • ₹ 120/- 5640 C • ₹ 120/- 5615 D • ₹ 150/- 8972 C • ₹ 80/- 4001 A • ₹ 150/- 5646 A • ₹ 225/- 4017 D • ₹ 150/-

PERSONALITY DEVELOPMENT

8748 E • ₹ 195/- | 9666 A • ₹ 150/- | 9678 R • ₹ 195/-

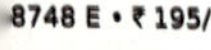    

9670 E • ₹ 240/- | 9696 M • ₹ 220/- | 9070 B • ₹ 195/-

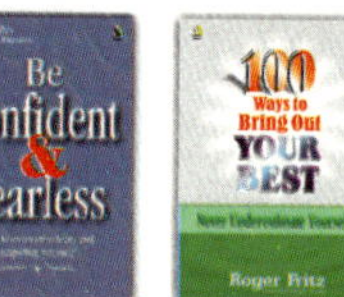 

9028 D • ₹ 175/- | 5641 A • ₹ 150/- | 9450 B • ₹ 195/-

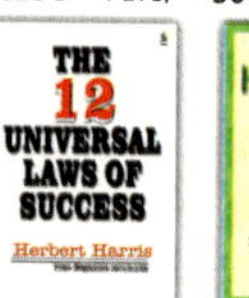   

9088 C • ₹ 195/- | 9667 B • ₹ 150/- | 8966 E • ₹ 100/-

5639 B • ₹ 80/- | 9466 T • ₹ 96/- | 9973 B • ₹ 110/-

9981 B • ₹ 96/- | 8868 D • ₹ 120/- | 9487 E • ₹ 150/-

STUDENT DEVELOPMENT

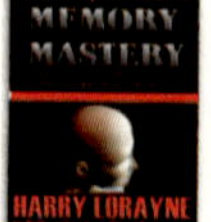    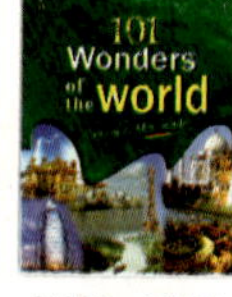

9090 A • ₹ 220/- | 9668 C • ₹ 150/- | 9071 D • ₹ 165/- | 8731 B • ₹ 100/- | 9495 R • ₹ 175/-

  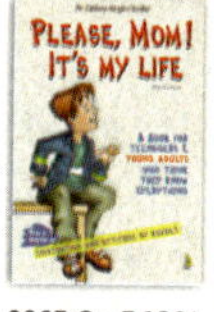

9455 C • ₹ 150/- | 5622 A • ₹ 120/- | 9967 C • ₹ 120/-

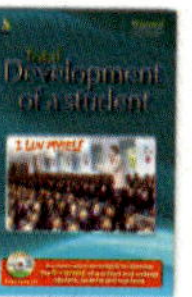

2241 J • ₹ 100/- | 94441 S • ₹ 195/- | 9654 D • ₹ 100/-

9652 D • ₹ 120/- | 8962 A • ₹ 150/- | 9089 D • ₹ 135/-

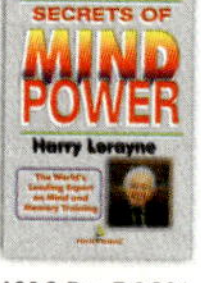  

4016 D • ₹ 160/- | 4009 K • ₹ 150/- | 8997 B • ₹ 120/-

4010 L • ₹ 100/- | 9787 P • ₹ 100/- | 2244 D • ₹ 80/-

PARENTING

9906 J • ₹ 250/- (HB) | 8261 D • ₹ 180/-

9674 J • ₹ 220/- | 9784 J • ₹ 150/-

9594 K • ₹ 80/- | 8917 D • ₹ 120/-

9458 G • ₹ 80/- | 9438 B • ₹ 150/-

9065 A • ₹ 80/- | 9994 E • ₹ 120/-

ALTERNATIVE THERAPIES

8882 F • ₹ 215/-

8983 E • ₹ 100/-

8836 D • ₹ 135/-

9935 F • ₹ 120/-

5637 D • ₹ 96/-

8889 D • ₹ 100/-

8842 D • ₹ 100/-

8941 A • ₹ 100/-

COMMON AILMENTS & DISEASES

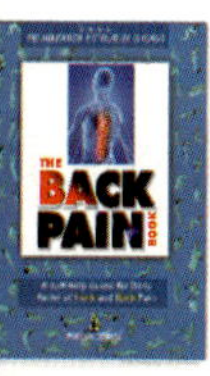

8891 D • ₹ 120/-

8281 A • ₹ 100/-

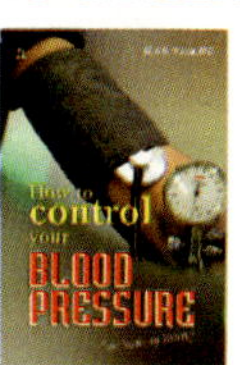

8094 D • ₹ 120/-

8848 D • ₹ 150/-

8276 A • ₹ 96/-

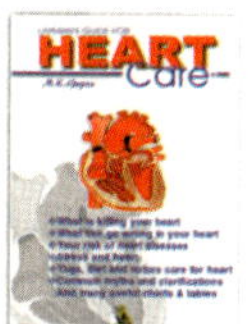

8888 D • ₹ 96/-

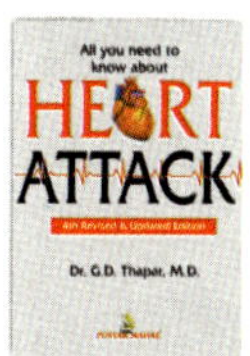

8908 D • ₹ 120/-

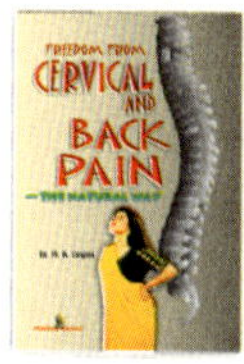

8878 B • ₹ 80/-

GENERAL HEALTH

9075 C • ₹ 225/-

8747 D • ₹ 150/-

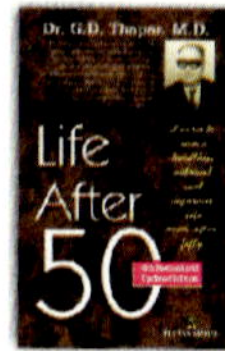

9940 D • ₹ 150/-

8859 G • ₹ 80/-

8877 A • ₹ 150/-

8847 M • ₹ 100/-

8870 D • ₹ 100/-

9950 B • ₹ 120/-

9902 F • ₹ 120/-

SLIMMING & FITNESS

8277 B • ₹ 120/-

8875 K • ₹ 120/-

9445 A • ₹ 150/-

DIET & NUTRITION

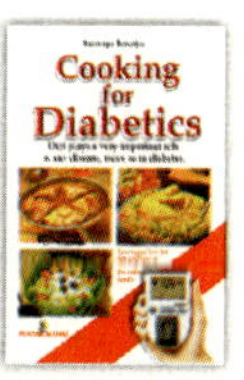

9941 D • ₹ 100/-

8904 D • ₹ 150/-

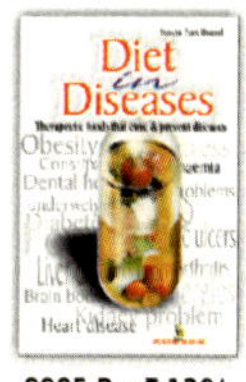

8985 B • ₹ 120/-

8968 G • ₹ 120/-

8271 C • ₹ 96/-

9037 D • ₹ 150/-

HINDOOLOGY / RELIGION / SPIRITUAL BOOKS

9873 C • ₹ 60/-

9770 E • ₹ 150/-

9453 A • ₹ 250/-

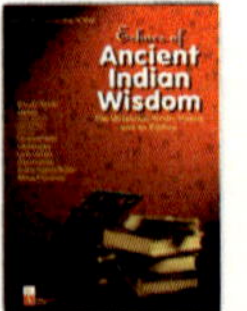
4179 A • ₹ 295/- (HB)

4138 B Rs. 250

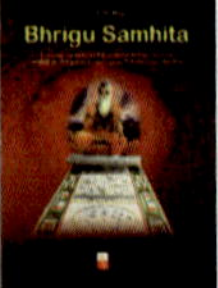
4177 B • ₹ 250/-

9997 C • ₹ 80/-

4181 C • ₹ 195/-

9984 E • ₹ 399/- (HB)

4130 B • ₹ 120/-

9811 P • ₹ 120/-

9585 A • ₹ 96/-

9508 D • ₹ 95/-

9989 D • ₹ 96/-

4183 A • ₹ 350/- (HB)

9504 D • ₹ 100/-

9540 D • ₹ 150/-

9513 A • ₹ 195/-

4126 B • ₹ 96/-

9812 R • ₹ 120/-

9504 D • ₹ 100/-

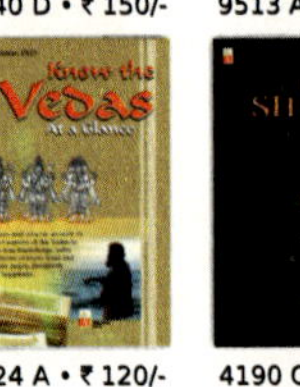
4124 A • ₹ 120/-

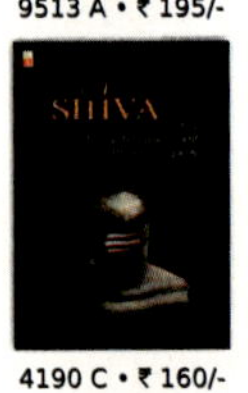
4190 C • ₹ 160/-

9509 A • ₹ 150/-

4152 B • ₹ 96/-

4188 A • ₹ 160/-

4132 D • ₹ 100/-

9987 E • ₹ 150/-

9520 D • ₹ 120/-

4134 B • ₹ 80/-

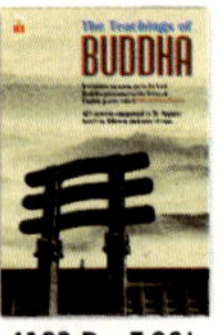
4182 D • ₹ 96/-

9405 A • ₹ 19

COMPUTERS

7712 K • ₹ 165/-

7711 J • ₹ 120

9768 C • ₹ 175/-

7766 A • ₹ 120

HOME MAKING / GRILLS & RAILIN

3111 E • ₹ 175/-

3107 F • ₹ 88

3106 E • ₹ 100/-

3105 D • ₹ 100

3108 G • ₹ 150/-

3104 M • ₹ 10

ASTROLOGY/VASTU/HYPNOTISM/PAMISTRY

9871 A • ₹ 240/-

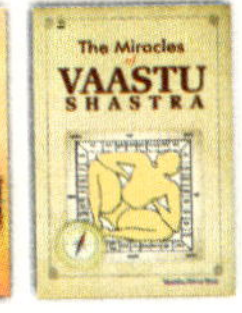

9693 H • ₹ 195/-

9671 F • ₹ 195/-

2127 D • ₹ 250/-

4177 C • ₹ 295/-

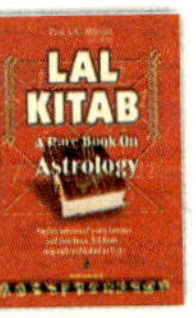

9086 A • ₹ 295/-HB

2116 D • ₹ 150/-

8259 D • ₹ 88/-

2109 F • ₹ 150/-

2112 D • ₹ 120/-

3110 B • ₹ 120/-

2133 B • ₹ 96/-

8899 D • ₹ 195/-

8925 D • ₹ 96/-

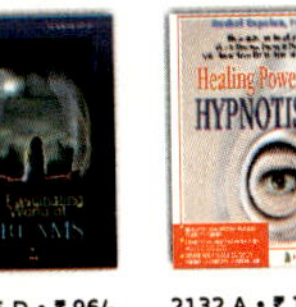

2132 A • ₹ 150/-

9432 D • ₹ 150/-

2120 D • ₹ 150/-

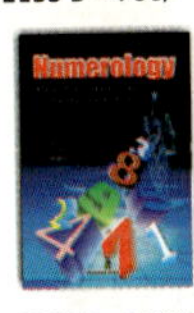

2109 F • ₹ 100/-

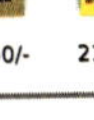

FICTION

Set Code SH 001

Set Code 9795 A

Set Code 9752 B • ₹ 550/-

ENGLISH IMPROVEMENT

97540 D • ₹ 175/-

5541 C • ₹ 196/-

6651 E • ₹ 195/-

9448 D • ₹ 175/-

9056 A • ₹ 125/-

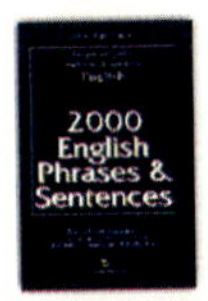

5538 D • ₹ 100/-

SAYING/QUOTATIONS/ PROVERBS

9474 F • ₹ 170/-

9789 A • ₹ 150/-

8999 D • ₹ 80/-

9953 A • ₹ 100/- 8947 E • ₹ 100/- 8890 D • ₹ 150

5512 A • ₹ 150/- 8963 B • ₹ 80/- 9425 A • ₹ 60

PERSON & PERSONALITIES

9669 D • ₹ 120/-

9825 E • ₹ 150/-

2113 D • ₹ 195/-

9764 R • ₹ 100/-

8991 D • ₹ 120/-

JOKES HUMOUR & SATIRE

2342 C • ₹ 100/- 2343 D • ₹ 100/-

2341 B • ₹ 96/- 2318 A • ₹ 96/-

2330 B • ₹ 96/- 2319 B • ₹ 96/-

BODY/BEAUTY CARE

8093 D • ₹ 150/-

9986 B • ₹ 150/-

8971 B • ₹ 120/-

9922 F • ₹ 120/-

8865 F • ₹ 120/-

FUN, FACTS, MAGIC & MYSTERIES

9484 B • ₹ 150/-

2275 D • ₹ 120/-

9479 M • ₹. 120/-

9470 B • ₹ 100/-

2208 M • ₹ 100/-

9816 D • ₹ 100/-

2247 F • ₹ 100/-

2250 A • ₹ 110/-

2211 F • ₹ 100/-

9457 E • ₹ 150/-

2237 M • ₹ 100/-

2335 A • ₹ 80/-

2243 L • ₹ 100/-

9775 M • ₹ 100/-

9985 A • ₹ 80/-

5110 A • ₹ 80/-

2337 C • ₹ 100/-

2336 B • ₹ 100/-

2331 C • ₹ 100/-

9977 B • ₹ 100/-

YOGA & MEDITATION

8269 A • ₹ 195/-

9998 D • ₹ 150/-

8939 D • ₹ 96/-

9958 S • ₹ 160/-

9087 B • ₹ 195/-

2118 F • ₹ 120/-

8901 D • ₹ 150/-

8099 D • ₹ 80/-

9025 D • ₹ 80/-

HOMEOPATHY, AYURDEDA

9446 B • ₹ 150/-

8887 D • ₹ 195/-

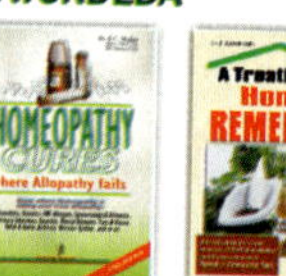

8270 B • ₹ 195/-

8923 D • ₹ 195/-

8010 D • ₹ 96/-

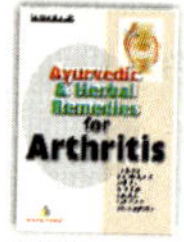

9094 E • ₹ 96/-

8944 D • ₹ 175/-

8948 A • ₹ 120/-

WORLD FAMOUS SERIES

9472 D • ₹ 100/-

5164 E • ₹ 100/-

9483 A • Rs. 100/-

51107 • ₹ 100/-

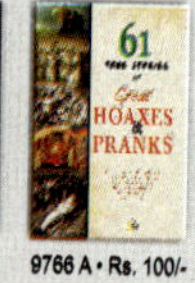

9766 A • Rs. 100/-

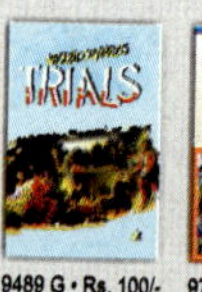

9489 G • Rs. 100/-

9761 M • Rs. 120/-

World Famous Mysterious Objects
True Stories of Mowglis and other Wild Childrens
World Famous Treasures (Lost and Found)
World Famous WARs & Battles
True Stories of Mystic Places
World Famous Adventures
World Famous Military Operations
World Famous Spy Scandals
World Famous Spies & Spymasters
World Famous Crooks & Con Men
True Stories 81 Weird Humans
True Stories of Great Explorers
World Famous Strange Mysteries
and many more.......

LOVE, ROMANCE & SEX

9602 B • Rs. 125/-

8260 D • Rs. 96/-

8266 D • Rs. 80/-

8278 C • Rs. 100/-

8916 D • Rs. 120/-

MORAL, WISDOM & FAIRY TALES

9677 P • Rs. 150/-

9486 D • Rs. 250/-

8967 F • Rs. 80/-

9077 E • Rs.120/-

9563 N • Rs. 125/-

2289 D • ₹ 96/-